A Soul Under Siege

A Soul Under Siege

SURVIVING CLERGY DEPRESSION

C. Welton Gaddy

Westminster/John Knox Press
Louisville, Kentucky

Book design by Ken Taylor

First edition

Published by Westminster/John Knox Press
Louisville, Kentucky

PRINTED IN THE UNITED STATES OF AMERICA
9   8   7   6   5   4   3   2   1

Library of Congress Cataloging-in-Publication Data

Gaddy, C. Welton.
    A soul under siege : surviving clergy depression / C. Welton Gaddy.—1st ed.
        p.   cm.
    ISBN 0-664-25211-7

    1. Gaddy, C. Welton. 2. Southern Baptist Convention—Clergy—Biography. 3. Baptists—United States—Clergy—Biography.
    4. Depression, Mental—Patients—United States—Biography.
    5. Clergy—Mental health—United States. I. Title.
BX6495.G27A3 1991
286′.1′092—dc20 [B]   91-2054

Dedicated to
Julia Mae (Judy) Grabiel Gaddy
John Paul Gaddy
James Welton Gaddy

Contents

Foreword

A teacher and mentor of mine, Spafford A. Ackerly, M.D., the late head and founder of the department of psychiatry of the University of Louisville, as a loyal Presbyterian once asked me, "Wayne, what do ministers do when they get depressed?"

"I guess they just plod along, because 'the show must go on.'"

And that is just what we are most likely to do. Or the depression impairs our judgment until we do some foolish, self-defeating things, and our work suffers badly as a result. No matter how many words of wise urging we receive suggesting that we slow down, quit carrying the world on our shoulders, and get adequate medical and psychiatric attention, we plod right on: "The show must go on."

Welton Gaddy, however, in *A Soul Under Siege,* a frank, considerate, and attention-keeping book, tells the story of how he stopped the show, entered a well-organized modern psychiatric unit, and received psychiatric care. He tells also of his discovery there of a more honest community in the hospital than he had ever known in churches. In fact, his comparison of the psychiatric unit with church life shows the deficiencies of the "show" people put on at church. He shows how the masks of sanity are laid aside in the group life of a well-organized psychiatric unit.

I have worked full time in three such units at this school of medicine for sixteen years. I can vouch for the fidelity to fact with which Welton Gaddy writes so lucidly. We have a motto we follow in our units: "You can be flaky as you want to here, but you can't get away with being fakey!"

I am privileged to have known Welton Gaddy as a fellow Christian pastor and as a colleague teaching in a seminary, but I am privileged most of all to have him as a friend who has honored me by being as candid with me as he is with you in *A Soul Under Siege*. He has had massive influence on generations of theological students and parishioners. Even while composing this foreword, I saw one of his former parishioners, who was a member of the Broadway Church in Fort Worth and who was ordained to the ministry while Welton was pastor there. He said of Welton, "I listened to him preach Sunday after Sunday and was empowered by the depth of what he had to say." He readily said that Welton was an important mentor for him.

Depression plagued the whole mature life of William Cowper, the hymn writer of many of our hymns such as "God Moves in a Mysterious Way His Wonders to Perform." A recent article in the *American Journal of Psychiatry* gives a full account of Cowper's pilgrimage, and chronicles with great empathy and reverence his faith in God and Christ. Clearly, the stereotypes of the godlessness of psychiatry are smashed by articles of this sort and pulverized by Welton Gaddy's *A Soul Under Siege*.

Inherent in Gaddy's book is the emergence of a long-lost kind of preaching and religious discourse—confessional preaching. John Bunyan did this in his immortal *Grace Abounding*. Anton Boisen did so in his *Out of the Depths*. John Claypool made a rich contribution to confessional preaching from his pulpit in his *Tracks of a Fellow Struggler*. Gaddy points out the worth of making ourselves vulnerable by sharing our own hearts, frustrations, and failures along with our few victories. A large segment of our church population wants "the show to go on," for the preacher to from

from behind his or her mask, to entertain them and make them feel momentarily good, until they hit the real world again. Fortunately, Gaddy's book shows the dangers of this perspective.

Gaddy's *A Soul Under Siege* is also a unique contribution to the growing literature of narrative theology. Each person has a story to tell. The Spirit of God working in us calls a person to his or her other place in life. The Spirit of God fills this story with the redemption and transformation of the earthen vessels that compose our lives. In creation God intended Welton Gaddy to be Welton Gaddy as he is, and nobody else. Gaddy shucks off the culturally imposed counterfeits of his ministry in this book. He fulfills Aristotle's dictum, "The rational mind is just what it is and nothing else." He also seems to be breathing Socrates' prayer: "O Lord, give me beauty in my inner soul, and let the outward person and inward person be the same."

Let me urge you, in the words of the *Book of Common Prayer*, to "read, mark, . . . and inwardly digest" this book.

WAYNE E. OATES

Preface

I am not certain that I want this book to be read. However, I have no question about my desire or need to write it.

Initially, I wrote most of the material in this volume for myself, with little thought of anyone else, other than my wife and our sons, ever seeing it. Often words flowed lucidly in a stream-of-consciousness fashion, and I recorded them quickly, as if driven to do so. Sometimes, though, expressions virtually had to be ripped from my psyche because to hold them in mind and to pen them on paper was to feel again the terrible pain that had been associated with them. The ordinarily hard work of writing was intensified immensely. Pondering thoughts to be set in paragraphs meant engaging memories of moments I had hoped could be forgotten.

Ambivalence has abounded from the inception of this project and has regularly disturbed my determination to complete it. In their earliest forms, some sections of this work were scribbled with an urgency akin to that which fills a doctor doing surgery to correct a patient's life-threatening heart condition. Other sections almost did not materialize at all because of my awareness that if, indeed, my writing was akin to a surgical procedure, I was operating on myself with a dull knife and questionable skills.

Originally I intended to address in writing the issues that appear in the first five chapters of this book. However, I could not dismiss the counsel of Davis Perkins, a respected editor with exemplary expertise, who urged me to lift from my experience insights and principles with a potential to be helpful to others. The last chapter represents my response to that idea.

Numerous times I have decided to pull back from the publication process. Frankly, I do not like to be this honest in revelations about myself in public. That does not mean I want to be dishonest; it means simply that in relation to many matters intensely personal in nature I prefer to be silent. Most likely private conversations with family members or with very close friends would have been the only context in which the bulk of this material ever would have been shared, if at all, had it not been for the strong encouragement of my wife, Judy, my friend Floyd Thatcher, and my editor, Davis Perkins, all of whom agreed on the possibility of others' being helped by these reflections on my hurt. Trusting their hope for helpfulness but continuing to feel a great deal of reticence, I completed the book.

Claiming the opportunity to state in print my appreciation for and gratitude to certain people has been by far the most pleasant part of the entire publication process. Kay Wilson Shurden and Walter B. (Buddy) Shurden are friends who have embraced both my wife and me as family members— not as distant cousins, but as brother and sister. When requested, these two talented people made us the beneficiaries of their professional skills. More importantly, in many ways, at their initiatives, Buddy and Kay gave expression to an unconditional loving acceptance, the experience of which for me often was like catching a deep breath of fresh, life-giving air just when breaths were coming in such short gasps that to breathe normally seemed an impossibility. Howard Bramlette and Joe Paul Pruett are highly adept authors of encouragement and harbingers of hope. Over the years, Floyd Craig and I have maintained a special friendship undeterred by (actually, strengthened by) the challenge of sharing problems. The fact that during the past several months on many days Floyd has made two or three long-distance phone calls to me is indicative of his innumerable efforts to be helpful. I am very grateful to and for all these people.

Two doctors did well what they get paid to do but also extended care in ways that were not billed. I am thankful for Mary Patton and Craig Johnson.

Throughout the period described in this book, no one person has been more important to me and more helpful to me than my wife, Judy. Her support has been as unrelenting as her love is unfailing. Judy has challenged me, questioned me, angered me, comforted me, and instructed me. Daily Judy has practiced more of the gospel than I have preached cumulatively across the years. With incredible resilience and courage, she has refused to allow me to forget how to laugh.

Sources of strength for both Judy and me are our two sons, John Paul and James. As can be deduced from the narrative on the pages that follow, for a sizable stretch of time these two young men have been asked to deal with difficulties which they did not create, to shoulder burdens which they did not deserve to have to carry, and to accept responsibilities that occasionally overloaded their already full days. I am thankful that, even during my most difficult times, James and John Paul treated me no differently than they had previously. Each continued to voice thoughts and feelings straightforwardly as well as to joke (often at my expense) rowdily. Neither one of them allows the other, Judy, or me to wonder about the strength of his love. Though both of our sons are uncomfortable with syrupy holy talk and ready at any moment with great laughter to label self-righteousness and piosity as what they are, each is a person possessing and possessed by a profound faith shot full of the biblically defined qualities of justice, grace, and hope. These fellows are greatly appreciated friends as well as much-loved sons.

This book is dedicated to my wife and our two sons (each

of whom has agreed that this story should be told), with the hope that the words on its pages can be in some measure as helpful to readers as the lives of these three people have been beneficial to the writer.

C.W.G.

Introduction: Bottoming Up

In the distance someone was picking at a piano. Pauses of silence, caused by an unpracticed amateur's search for the proper keys, interspersed various musical notes being banged out in such a fashion as faintly to suggest some semblance of the melody of a Christmas carol. "Joy to the World." "Silent Night." Surely not here. Not now. No way. Where I sat listening to this semirhythmic racket seemed about as far removed from a holy night, about as distant from an advent of the Divine that would cause heaven and nature to sing, as earth from sky. I was a new patient in the mental-health unit of a large metropolitan medical facility. I was anxious. I was depressed. I was hurting.

Recent history could be remembered mostly as a blur. It seemed as if I had felt fatigue forever. For months I had procrastinated on responsibilities usually dispatched with immediacy. Deadlines were missed. Letters were unanswered. Phone calls were not returned. Decisions were delayed. That lifelong, relentless drive toward tireless activities aimed at getting everything done immediately had been replaced by an indefinable though aggressive preoccupation which deadened initiative and distorted judgment, which prevented getting much of anything done, ever. To be sure, I was unaware of the radicalism of that inner change. But it did not matter. I did not care. For the first time in my life, I did not seem to care much about anything. I had no sense of what had happened to me or of its significance for me. Who was playing that Christmas music?

Event after event had eroded my self-confidence and jeopardized my sense of security. First, during a quickly scheduled appointment, my medical doctor diagnosed high blood pressure as the cause of a three-week-long headache. She spoke with frightening sternness of the necessity for me to reduce the outer stress in my life and to make the kind of changes in my lifestyle that would lower the dangerous level of hypertension that threatened a stroke or a heart attack. I was reeling. Health always had been a major source of pride for me, never a problem in any way. What was going on?

Second, a series of poor judgments and bad decisions related to ministry had raised serious questions regarding my extant ability to function effectively as a minister. Hearing the articulation of those questions from respected friends was tremendously disturbing, even disorienting. Typically the feedback to my ministry had been overwhelmingly positive in nature. Big words that I cherished as affirmations of character included integrity, competence, excellence, courage, trustworthiness, and effectiveness. What had happened?

On the Wednesday afternoon following Thanksgiving weekend, after returning home from a trip to reclaim my car, which had been stolen the previous week (a real stress reducer!), my wife and a good friend greeted me with the news that all the arrangements had been made for me to check into a hospital because of the presence of the dangerous hypertension as well as a high level of stress and a continuing depression. My bag already was packed. I did not argue. I looked across the room at our older son, and he nodded at me with an encouraging look. At that moment, I trusted the judgment of these people far more than my own.

I did ask how and why the decision had been made. My wife explained that earlier in the day, while I was away, she had shared her concern about me with three of our closest friends. Subsequently, two of them consulted with the medical doctor who had diagnosed the hypertension. Then all of them concluded that hospitalization for rest and therapy was in my best interest. In the meantime, my physician also wrote to one of the leaders in our church indicating my need for a medical leave of absence. Too much was happening at far too fast a pace for me to get a handle on it. I simply had to trust the inclinations of my family and friends. After all, I had no question that these people were motivated by a love for me and a heartfelt commitment to do what was best.

One of my few reservations about the decision for hospitalization was rooted in the realization that the depth of my depression in the past had been greater than the depression I felt at the moment. However, I had no way accurately to assess my needs.

The one-and-one-half-hour drive to the hospital was filled with questions about responsibilities to be reassigned and people to be contacted, uneasiness, anxiety, nervous chatter, and laughter akin to the high-strung whistling that accompanies a brisk walk through a graveyard at night.

Admission into the hospital was quick and easy. All the necessary arrangements had been handled adeptly by a friend. Relief born of a smooth entry soon was replaced by shock. Silently my two companions and I followed directional signs to the mental-health unit, down a long, sterile-looking hall to an electronically controlled door which served as the entrance to the mental-health unit for those on the outside and as a barrier to the outside world for those on the inside. Oh, the scenes were all familiar. Over the years, I had been in countless units like this one—but always as a pastor, a care-giver, never as a patient, a recipient of care. What in God's name was I doing here? I knew well the kinds of people who occupy these wards. Surely I am not one of them, I thought. Or am I?

What came next has been the source of hearty laughs when viewed in retrospect. When the nurse came to get me for an orientation session, she looked at the three of us standing awkwardly in the hall and asked, "Which one is the patient?" Don't think I ever will allow my wife and my friend to forget that laugh-producing question. But at that moment no one was laughing. Told that the intake interview and orientation would require at least an hour, I hesitantly said good-bye to my wife and friend.

Suddenly, all the people I knew were gone. But that was not all. Gone as well was the professional-social world I knew so thoroughly, and with it the security-enhancing value of all my time-tested skills for expressing self-assertion, making small talk, masquerading feelings, helping with confrontation, and pushing toward success. Never before had I been in this place, geographically or emotionally. Previously unknown feelings rushed to the forefront of my awareness.

A good portion of that particular morning, much like that of any Wednesday, had been spent thinking about the subject matter for a meditation I would be expected to deliver to our church people in that evening's prayer service. As I looked at my watch, I realized the hour for me to speak had arrived. But a homily was not in order. I was not even with the people in our church. Instead, I sat across the desk from a perfect stranger with whom I was beginning to share thoughts and feelings I never had expressed to anyone—not even to those whom I loved most. In fact, I had been conditioned to believe that the protection of complete privacy by way of the repression of certain ideas and emotions was a sign of strength.

Only the day before all this disturbing, disruptive turbulence, much of my attention had centered on the Sunday immediately ahead—the first Sunday of Advent, one of my favorite times in the Christian year. With great enthusiasm I had started to write the sermon for that day. The manuscript never was completed. I had assumed there would be plenty of time for more writing later in the week. Little did I know!

Incidentally, the subject of that sermon was hope—hope—a spiritual gift easily recognizable during Advent, a gift from God, a gift I would need to receive not just during Advent but again and again. That Wednesday evening I sat for a long while on top of the uncomfortable, plastic-covered bunk bed that occupied most of the space in my new home. My thoughts and emotions fluctuated rapidly, rising and falling, comforting and disturbing, demanding full attention and subsiding without notice.

As I look back on that occasion, the next item of my recall involves the distant sounds produced by the shoddy piano player, the captivating, even if barely discernible, melody of a Christmas carol. 'Tis the season to be jolly! Now is the time for singing angels, the ringing of bells, and a reverberation of cosmic hallelujahs. But not here. Not this year. Not now. Suddenly I wished I had finished writing the sermon on hope, even though I knew I would not be preaching the coming Sunday. I needed to know what I would have written. Hope is one thing when a subject for elaboration by someone sitting at the desk in an office or a topic of proclamation as one stands behind the pulpit in a sanctuary, but it is something else altogether as a gift in need of recognition and reception as one tries to get comfortable in one of the stark cubicles of a mental-health facility. Or is it? I had to find out.

During my intake interview and logistical orientation to the unit, I found myself trying to do at least two things at once. I never have been any good at that and was not this time. In the consultation room, I answered a series of questions that ranged from requests for perfunctory information to inquiries aimed at establishing deep-seated feelings and identifying perceived problems. While walking around in the hospital facility, I nodded mechanically and muttered thoughtlessly as responses to instructions about where to pick up laundry, where to find snacks, how to operate the television, and the like. All the while I was trying to think through the matters of most interest to me.

Admittedly, my first thoughts were by no means the most important thoughts. Often interests are unrelated to importance. How will the church be told about my hospitalization? What will people think of me? Will persons whom I have counseled understand my need for counsel? Will this episode of seeking care throw into question my competence? Will hospitalization for hypertension, stress, and depression jeopardize future opportunities for ministry? I knew well the kinds of compassionate thoughts I had experienced in relation to other people in similar situations. But I wondered if that would be the nature of thoughts formed about me. Will the church act like the church or revert to a position predictable for any social unit that places institutional concerns over interest in individuals?

Had I been thinking clearly, I would have met this whole intimidating onrush of issues of self-interest with a quick "So what?" Most important at the moment were rest and recovery—not the judgments of others, the subjects of rumors, or the actions of a congregation. If I did not get better, none of that would matter anyway. If I did get better, I could deal with each of those concerns appropriately. Sufficient for the hour were the love of family members, the support of friends, and the resourcefulness of faith. I had to concentrate on getting help.

Eventually my grappling with the situation resulted in some positive developments. I realized that I had to set aside a professional identity (which can be a mask behind which to hide emotionally) with all of its stereotypical concern with piety, willpower, stability, strength, and wisdom and allow myself to be a patient with problems, fears, and needs. Actualizing that realization was a constant struggle.

I resolved to give my full attention to the clinical situation, whether or not I liked it. That meant letting down barriers to openness, sitting and talking with other patients, spending time with therapists, taking advantage of every group session, and joining community activities. My ability for such an unprotected interaction increased with every passing day of hospitalization.

I focused on the need for honesty. Like others, I am sure, I had been accustomed to hiding hurts, disguising disappointments, guarding against any revelation of a mood of despondency, and even covering up natural physical ailments so as to be able to answer every "How are you?" with a "Just fine" and to present the image of a nearly perfect minister who is a "tower of strength."

As my attitude changed, my agenda was altered—stepping down from a professional pedestal, dismantling defensiveness, admitting needs, praying for help, pledging emotional honesty, requesting counsel. I became less disturbed about discovering other people's thoughts about me and more concerned about better understanding myself. Instead of trying to devise a way to come out of all this looking good, I focused my efforts on learning from critiques, studying constructive suggestions, and giving myself without reservation to a process aimed at improved health. The result was my eventual dismissal from the hospital with greater clarity of thought and more stability in emotions than I had known in eight to ten years, as well as the discovery of a sense of inner calm and a peaceful hope about the long-term future.

None of this came easily. (Even writing about it is difficult.) At times the diverse pulls on my psyche and multiple tugs at my soul were cyclonic in nature. More than once, giving up seemed much preferable to carrying on. Any relief that came from a diagnosis of my situation was quickly replaced by anxiety and fears spawned by the difficulties and time demands related to coping with and improving this situation. Who wants to hear: "You are depressed. You probably have been depressed for several years. Getting better quite possibly can require at least two years of therapy"? Not me.

Not yet (if ever) can I declare that everything will come out

all right. It is too soon to know. In fact, that is one of the
drawbacks of setting down these thoughts at this time. I
realize that chronological distance from events can contribute to a more accurate perspective on the events. However, I
am willing to risk the disadvantages involved in writing
about this dark night of the soul too soon rather than to risk
losing touch with the profound intensity and complexity of
the thoughts, emotions, and issues that were and are so
much a part of it.

Why write anything at all? To be honest, my motives are
mixed. Writing about a situation is beneficial to me in terms
of analysis and prognosis. I am a merchant of words. Almost
every week I exercise the discipline of attempting to translate
into understandable language mystical matters of faith,
unspeakable components of tragedy, depths of emotions
that defy explanations, horrendous doubts more akin to
destructive storms than to rational confessions, pleas for
help suitable for sobs and screams but not correctly struc-
tured sentences, and beliefs about seemingly nonsensical
hope. I find great help in working at the best verbal
description of difficulties, wrestling with words that capture
realistic alternative responses, and pondering the phrases
that most accurately convey my convictions and intentions.
So what follows is as much for me as for anyone else.

I am well aware, though, that a careful tracing of one's
own experience can prove helpful to other people trying to
make their ways through similar circumstances. That somewhat shaky hunch has hardened into a firm conviction as I
have read letter after letter and listened to phone call after
phone call in which people have poured out to me their
kinship in pain and encouraged me to share in writing
anything that might facilitate greater understanding of such
a crisis among observers, if not offer help in moving them,
those involved, toward meaningful solutions. Certainly I
would like to think that my struggle has not been without
some benefit that can be shared with others as well as
claimed by myself. This is not to imply that any two

situations are alike or that I have dealt with my difficulties in an exemplary manner. Knowing, however, that I have profited greatly from written accounts of the pilgrimages of others, I find myself hoping that someone can find at least minimal assistance from my reflections.

My purpose in these pages is not to produce a scholarly treatise on depression, stress, anxiety, and their predictable companions. Library shelves are filled with excellent volumes that examine these issues with great medical, psychological, and spiritual expertise. I am writing as a patient, not as a doctor. Carefully honed, clinically accurate definitions of the various components of trauma are not my concern. I want to share only what I personally have felt, thought, feared, and hoped. The material that follows is absolutely subjective. The sources of most of these words are not professional manuscripts but personal experiences—mine.

Outside of a setting for formal consultation, I have never heard many people declare, "I am depressed" or "I hurt." Just the opposite, really. Factor in my identity as a minister and the sparsity of honest confessions of needs looks more like a radical scarcity, an absolute rarity. I could have been helped immensely merely by reading of or hearing from someone whom I respect admitting fatigue, depression, or some similar difficulty. If the statement had come from a person of faith, it would have been all the more forceful.

Studies in emotional disorders document the pervasiveness of the phenomenon of depression among many greatly admired historical figures as well as highly revered biblical personalities. But general knowledge was of little personal help.

Vaguely, I recalled that two of my heroes struggled with depression. Though I could not remember the specifics, I knew that in his autobiography Harry Emerson Fosdick had written candidly about his long bout with depression, and that all who write about Martin Luther note the depression that was his lifelong enemy.

For Luther, depression was chronic. The little monk from

Wittenberg interpreted his emotional struggle as positively as possible, labeling depression as a major positive factor in his preparation for the Christian ministry. Yet, after one extended episode of depression, Luther confessed, "I was close to the gates of death and hell."

Biographers of Harry Emerson Fosdick write of his experience with "a severe neurotic reactive depression," which required a four-month stay in a New York sanitarium plus an additional expanse of time for recuperation. At one point in what Fosdick called "the most hideous experience in my life," despair led this mighty messenger of the good news to place a razor to his throat.

Both Luther and Fosdick were persons of profound faith, from whose ministries I have benefited significantly. Their words help. Periodically, I need to be reassured that redemptive faith is not a prophylactic unconditionally guaranteed to prevent an impregnation with worry, panic, guilt, depression, and other such negative feelings as futility, purposelessness, and meaninglessness. If recording my words about emotional difficulties and critical events can help meet the same kind of need in others, I will be pleased.

Only a day or two after my release from the hospital I began trying to write about recent experiences. The task was much more difficult than I had imagined it would be. My good friend Floyd Thatcher urged me not to cease my efforts, encouraging me to grapple with my personal experiences in writing apart from any concern for format or publication possibilities. I was not sure I could do it, especially if there was a chance that at some time in the future someone else might see it. I never have been good at laying out my innards for examination by others. Floyd was very comforting and reassuring. His advice corresponded with the subsequent counsel of other trusted friends and concerned family members. Judy, my wife, applauded the idea of a writing project about the problem-saturated past and supported my efforts helpfully, though, knowing me well, she expressed caution regarding my tendency to repress or cover up thoughts and feelings that I dislike.

Not often do I trust others more than myself. But that too is changing. Over the past several months, I have listened carefully to many of my peers. At times I have found real pleasure and fulfillment in following directions given by persons whom I trust. What follows in this narrative is a form of satisfying obedience.

One other possibility must be noted as an explanation for the exercise that has resulted in these pages. What I know best is how to work. (That is no boast offered to elicit commendation, only an accurate confession.) Unfortunately, work has been my vocation, avocation, hobby, and means of relaxation (at least in my previous poorly arranged priorities). During the month following my hospitalization I offered my resignation to the church I was serving as pastor. For the first time in almost thirty years I was unemployed. Never before had I resigned from a position without knowing precisely what I would do next. Relief—welcome relief which the doctors had promised—was mingled with unwelcome fears, insecurity, and a sense of personal worthlessness, deprived as I was of financially remunerative work. I scrambled to find ways to use my "time off" productively, thinking that only in that manner could I justify days devoid of familiar routines. Thus the very accumulation of words in this book may serve as further evidence that I have not yet extracted myself from a work ethic which I have experienced as a problem while continuing to praise it as a blessing.

In a sense, I hope you can read this work without understanding my feelings or identifying with my words. If so, perhaps that will indicate you never have been before where I have been recently. Maybe you never will find yourself in such a situation. I wish that for you. But if you read with understanding and identification, if some of my journey coincides with your pilgrimage, then I hope you will sense a partnership in pain, an assurance that you are not alone. That is important. Many times I have wondered if anyone else had ever felt the way I did. Can any other person possibly understand my sentiments? To know you are not alone is to find a modicum of comfort.

This is not a how-to book—how to deal with depression, how to handle stress, how to overcome anxiety. I have not handled those problems very well experientially. Probably I could write about them theoretically. I am not audacious enough, however, for such an attempt. Neither is this volume an expression of pop psychology optimistically offered as a source of help for the masses, what I have learned that every person on the street should know.

Depression is a disorder with more potential causes than its obvious multiple symptoms. Each source of depression deserves serious attention. Professional help is needed. Every person must deal with depression on an individual basis, and under the guidance of a skilled physician embark on a course of treatment that may involve medication, psychotherapy, or lifestyle alterations, or, as with many people, all of these simultaneously. Depression can be treated with good results. But depression cannot be ignored without devastating consequences.

Whether or not what follows will be helpful to others, I really do not know. My only claim of value for this material relates to candor. Here is one person's experience, my experience, offered with the desire that a candid retelling of it can help those who have experienced, are confronting, or will face a bottoming-out moment in their lives to so deal with their situation that they will turn it around, thus transforming it into a time of bottoming up. Of course, I will not be disappointed if those who read my words discover within them fragments of a faith that remains confident of light even when everything is in darkness, and thereby hints at hope.

1

Exploding Myths and Facing Facts

"Reality doesn't matter." The church officer, deadly serious, was talking about a potentially disruptive situation in our congregation. He could just as easily have been a public relations expert, a fund-raiser, a corporate sales director, or the CEO in a major industry of any description. No one has a monopoly on such thought. Apparently that mentality exists in epidemic proportions. "Perception *is* reality." At stake was the idea that in a difficult dilemma, the highest priority is to deal with what people think is true regardless of what is actually true.

Immediate internal rumblings should have been interpreted as warning signals of a major danger. However, I nodded my head in agreement with this well-meaning friend. In our society the show's the thing. If business is booming and lines charting sales are running upward off the graph, what does it matter if the salespeople are coming apart at the seams because of stress? As long as the church is doing well institutionally—good attendance, attractive programs, adequate offerings, new members to report—there is no need to address the hell that ministerial staff members are experiencing personally. If a family appears happy in public, few onlookers will bother to consider what kind of strife and worry the members of that family are facing privately.

Conventional wisdom declares, "If it looks good, it is good," whatever the "it" is. Unfortunately, the converse conclusion is also held uncritically: "If it looks bad, it is bad."

I cannot believe I bought into that thought even for a second. But I did. Of course, I had done my share of commerce with that philosophy as a minister. I knew all too well what it was like to sit in a committee meeting outwardly calm and collected but inwardly disturbed and ready to scream, "Please deal with something important! Let's move from a preoccupation with show to a consideration of substance." But the very nature of my participation seemed to underscore the power and importance of the posture to which I was adamantly opposed. I did not scream. Rather, I conducted business so efficiently and perfunctorily that I looked like a good administrator. On their way out the door of the conference room at the conclusion of the meeting, committee members said, "Good meeting, pastor. Thanks for your expert assistance." Looking good was important, more important than I wanted to admit.

More than once I have stood in a pulpit and delivered a sermon in a style that exuded confidence and authority, some would even say power, while my mind was confused, my rubbed-raw emotions hurt like third-degree burns, and my spiritual life seemed to be sagging severely, on the verge of hitting bottom and splintering into a thousand pieces. Each time I have experienced this in a service, I have gone back to my office with compliments ringing in my ears and the self-assuring thoughts: It is good that they could not see how I actually was feeling. For the sake of the church, I am glad that all appeared to go well. That is best. Was it?

Granted, when perception is positive and reality is more negative, most of us can be bought off quite easily by perception. After all, who likes to look at negatives? Besides, many of us have a great capacity for denial. As long as negatives are not readily visible and what is on the surface looks good, with little effort we can convince ourselves that everything is all right. A perception that all is well is a major intoxicant which can help us at least escape reality even when it does not enable us to deny reality completely.

Yes, I bought the perception-is-reality pitch. For a while. But it did not last long. Maybe that line of thought can work organizationally, bureaucratically, institutionally. It cannot work individually, personally, relationally. Eventually moments of truth come, good or bad. Then, only reality counts (as if that has not been the case all along). We have to deal with reality ready or not.

My track record is pretty good. The most important sections on my résumé document enough accomplishments to be impressive. I have led many of the right conferences, lectured in enviable settings, served on the proper boards, traveled to romantic places, authored a diversity of materials, and worked for revered employers. I was busy, always. With little difficulty I could respond to a "How's it going?" with a "Well. It's going well," and be believable. But I had become uncomfortable with that answer. I knew better. Though hidden from others, some stark, unpleasant truths were becoming apparent to me.

For the past decade I have worked harder than ever before at facing facts, dealing with reality, confronting truth. However, as I look back now, sometimes I think the more diligently I sought to face reality, the less successful I was in that effort. Actually, the trek has been erratic—one step forward, five steps backward, three forward. Finally, though, a monumental and inescapable moment of truth arrived.

My days always have held enough opportunities for diversions should any serious self-centered thoughts about undesirable truths develop. Except for a brief stay after oral surgery, I had never before been a hospital patient. Then, suddenly, I was checking into a hospital for an unprescribed length of time, becoming a patient in a mental-health unit. Protected time for thinking seriously about myself, facing facts, confronting reality, discovering truths—these were no longer on-again, off-again options. These activities were the essential items on my mandated agenda for every day. I could not go dashing off to give attention to some more important ministerial matter. Every avenue of escape was blocked—no call that had to be returned immediately, no visit to make within the hour, no appointment waiting for attention, not even a sermon to write. I had to look at myself honestly.

Had I tried to dodge the issue at this point, I would have failed. On my first full day in the hospital, I met with a psychotherapist who was intent in his resolve to assist me in a confrontation with truth. Two registered nurses trained in mental-health services told me that I would meet with them at least once each day and once each night to talk about my thoughts, feelings, needs, and related concerns. Also, I began a series of excellent sessions with a psychiatrist skilled in testing and evaluation.

As I took test after test, no opportunity existed to ask, "What do most people say about this?" or "Is my choice of answers in conformity with the majority of responses that you receive?" Here, all that mattered was what I thought, decided, and said. I did a lot of squirming in my chair. Question after question made me probe into the past as well as into the present and detail for the doctor basic ideas, behavioral patterns, strengths, weaknesses, problems, anxieties, and values. Try as I might, I could not shift the subject of our dialogue to someone else. Myths had to be exploded and truths discovered.

A minor incident made me more aware of the major task to which I had to give myself. On the Monday morning preceding Wednesday's admission to the hospital, following a nerve-racking meeting on Sunday evening, I had posed for a picture requested by a publisher of one of my books. Instructions specified that the portrait was to be casual, informal, relaxed. As I rushed out of my office to meet the photographer, my mind was still on the gut-wrenching conversations I had recently been involved in. The camera does not, did not, lie. Since my hospitalization prevented me from following up on this matter, my secretary and my wife selected the pose to be forwarded to the publisher. My wife brought a copy of that picture to the hospital. When I looked at it, fright forced a gasp. I had no idea I looked so bad. My wife explained that on the print for publication the photographer had been able to remove some of the heaviest lines of stress on my face. Little comfort. I was embarrassed by the thought that anyone would see a snapshot of me in that condition. (The show's the thing!) The realization that a recent picture of me did not look familiar even to me made me more certain than before that for a significant length of time I had not looked at myself realistically. That had to be done.

The issue of facing facts was by no means settled in the hospital. Previous efforts at this endeavor were intensified. I did receive some helpful tools as well as constant encouragement to look at myself realistically. But this task is not easily learned or quickly, if ever, concluded. Daily I continue to work at separating myths from reality, illusions from truths, and fact from fiction.

Though most likely every profession has its inherent hindrances to dealing with reality, the ministry seems overloaded in that regard. In addition to the untruths about one's self with which every person must painfully come to grips at some time or other, a minister constantly has to resist the unrealistic expectations that well-intentioned people tend to assign to a person of his or her calling. Believe me, it is easy to allow other people to define reality for you when you always come out the better for it—admirable, wise, and heroic. These people seem so wise. More than once I have been caught up in others' opinions about me, totally unrealistic though they were, to the extent that I refused to be confused by facts. But facts come.

In the pages that follow are five statements of reality about myself. Each one is juxtaposed with an unrealistic but adulatory comment about myself from others. None is unique to me. Similar statements of exaltation have been heard by most every minister as well as by other persons in places of service and authority.

Ministers are people who do ministry. Most essential in that observation is the recognition that ministers are people, persons. Thus, people who are ministers are not unlike people who are involved in other activities and professions. Though the nuances of specific situations vary because of contexts, assumptions, and expectations, ministers must deal with the same kinds of problems that confront other people. And people who are not ministers cannot escape most of the potentially destructive pressures encountered by their church-related peers. At issue here are dangerous dimensions of the *human* condition. Thus, what follows is by no means a grappling with reality unique to ministers. No one is exempt from the siren songs of mythology—whether the enticing invitations to unreality are sung to a holy tune or to a secular melody.

My problem was a preference for uncritically accepting and readily believing such glowing generalizations. That made more difficult than ever the task of discovering important truths about myself. These five observations are shared with the hope of benefiting any reader in pursuit of realistic self-understanding.

REAL HUMANITY
"You are just incredible; totally unreal."

A question from several years ago has lingered in my mind. During an interview with a reporter covering a conference at which I was speaking, I was asked, "What do you know now that you did not know, and maybe wish you had known, earlier in your ministry?" Typically, when dealing with a reporter, responses are formed slowly and deliberately. This time was different. Immediately I said, "I realize that I am a human being."

That was the right answer. (Actually no other option ever existed. A human being is all I could be.) That such a profound, but simple, recognition came so late in life may be surprising. But that was the case. In fact, the ease and language with which I responded to the reporter's question in no way evidenced the problems, stress, and trauma that had accompanied my pilgrimage to that realization. However, I knew all too well the extreme importance of my statement and the high price that I had paid for the ability to make it.

As a college student, when I spoke in various places— local church services of worship, retreats, encampments— almost invariably someone would say to me, "You are the best I have ever heard," or "You are going to be the next Billy Graham." Unfortunately, I believed all such well-intended but overexaggerated remarks. Who does not want an exalted self-image?

Throughout my years of postgraduate education I encountered many excellent teachers who challenged the unrealistic expectations of their students and established as incontrovertible truth the real humanity of every individual. I listened, took notes, and understood. But the fruits of my learning were acknowledged much more in regard to others than applied to myself. I had believed my parents, who told me I was special. I had misinterpreted the gracious compliments of various people as evidence that I was not like everyone else.

With rushes of embarrassment, I recall certain incidents during seminary days—bungled opportunities for greater self-understanding. Once, in a preaching class, my beloved professor John Carlton spoke of the struggle involved in sermon preparation, the "burden of the pulpit." From the history of homiletics he took as examples of this truth renowned preachers who had written or spoken of the pain they experienced in their pulpit ministries. I was untouched. Why, I even questioned whether something must have been wrong with these preachers. Later, I told Dr. Carlton of my disagreement with his discussion of difficulties related to preaching. Surely I did not, but I honestly think I told him how easy preaching was for me. Little did I know!

With real regrets I call to mind again some of the insensitive feelings and simplistic, if not moralistic, judgments I made regarding the actions of some character in a case study or maybe even the behavior of a professor or a classmate. To hear someone talk of bad decisions or immoral actions as indications of a person's humanity made me cringe. That seemed like a light excuse for a heavy concern. I even had trouble with those individuals who, in response to a person with problems, mouthed the cliché, "There but for the grace of God go I." Not me! I thought. I know better. I'm not about to make such a blunder. You can be a human being without all of that.

My first encounter with "confessional preaching" came while listening to and reading the sermons of John Claypool—a professor, pastor, and community leader in Louisville, Kentucky, who later became a colleague and a friend there and still later my immediate predecessor as the senior minister at a church in Fort Worth, Texas. John never attempted to disguise the real humanity of the persons treated in a biblical text or a sermon illustration or to dodge the dilemmas of his own humanity. He talked a great deal about struggling, grieving, doubting, and hurting. For me, his honesty gave authenticity to his ministry. Though I can hardly believe it now, I remember times of thinking, I never have hurt like that; I have no pain to share. Incredibly, I mused, I wish I had some serious problems to discuss in my preaching.

Needless to say, things changed. In this area, my life seemed to make up for lost time with breakneck speed. Quickly I came to know struggle, weariness, doubt, criticism, disappointment. Often sermons were a pain to prepare. Sundays seemed to come more often than any other day of the week. I made mistakes, used bad judgment, came to senseless conclusions. Behavior I had criticized in others, I repeated myself. Of course, I was no more spared the negative consequences of negative actions than anyone else. I hurt. At times, I hurt badly. My humanity became for me an absolute certainty, a certainty born with no little difficulty.

As I began to get in touch with my humanity and lose the fear that recognizing humanity's effect on faith would be synonymous with denying the power of faith, I resolved not to dodge this issue any more. I tried to be straightforward in my implementation of this resolution. A recognition of the pervasiveness of personal hurt became an integral factor in my proclamation. In pastoral care, judging people's actions by a set of absolutist standards became far less important than introducing them to grace and pointing them toward redemption. Personally, I became far more self-revealing in relation to my own weaknesses, questions, fatigue, and failures.

While a truthful confrontation with my own real humanity was essential for me, such was not the preference of all others, especially some parishioners. After a sermon in which I spoke of my often unsuccessful struggles to live by the truths in the biblical text for the day, a choir member let me know that he did not want to hear of my difficulties with discipleship. This young man wanted a minister that "has it all together," a minister who can serve as a model and even be viewed on a pedestal. Just recently I once again conversed with such a mentality and questioned its realism. After I pointed to persons in the church who appreciated a candor with which they could identify, this bristly, self-appointed protector of perfection in the pulpit admitted a double standard. "We don't expect you, our minister, to be like the rest of us."

Please understand, I no more perfected a posture of complete candor regarding my humanity than I had successfully denied it. I could allow others a glimpse of my real self, but I was careful always to retreat into privacy for the kind of moments of self-revelation that could be devastating. I became very adept at allowing people to see just enough of my dark side to praise my honesty while hiding from people all my true feelings, lest they reject me. In other words, I found yet another means of perpetuating an attractive image of an exemplary minister that covered the ugliness of my real humanity. I loved to hear the remark, "You are so unique. I have never known a minister to be so honest." Humility was proving to be a major stepping-stone to superiority.

It would seem that awareness should improve experience after a while. Not so. Through the years I have continued to fluctuate between a recognition of what I know is my real humanity and a conjecture that maybe I actually am a little different in that regard. Facing up to my capacity for evil—a fact of life for authentic human beings—is not nearly so compelling a task, so pleasurable a pursuit, as speculating that most of the laws and rules meant to regulate the behavior of others do not apply to me because of my special messianic mission to others. Such is the power of denial.

Denying one's humanity is fraught with obvious dangers. Yet I still am susceptible to being seduced, at least temporarily, by comments of adulation, affirmation, and respect. "O Pastor, you are so wonderful!" "I have never known a person like you." Always, always, such remarks cause the surmise: Maybe she is right. Perhaps he knows me better than I know myself. I guess I could be that great. Looking to the future, I pray that in all such moments I may have the sensitivity to be nice to the person making the remark, the wisdom to allow a smile to cross my face, and the honesty quickly to say to myself, Don't you believe it. Don't you believe it for even one second.

REAL LIMITATIONS
"You can do anything you set out to do."

When the American dream is baptized by religion, and its promise of an open-ended future is theologically personalized, the individual involved may be victimized by unrealistic expectations which almost assure a harsh, even hurtful, confrontation with truth at some later point. Fantasy can be confused with faith. Totally unrealistic agendas for work can be praised as admirable intentions for mission. That is pretty much my story.

As a child, most of us (sad to say, excluding little girls until recently) found encouragement in personal applications of the Horatio Alger saga. Who knows also the long-term influence of the limits-defying characters of the cartoon superheroes who suggested we might move "faster than a speeding bullet" and "leap tall buildings in a single bound"? "You can be the President of the United States." Perhaps such statements kept many of us from setting our sights too low. For me, additional help came from friends who affirmed my worth, acknowledged the value of my personal gifts, and encouraged all efforts toward excellence. But when well-intended affirmations that aid the development of a child are carried over into adulthood as uncritically examined statements of fact, they can be very harmful. A major mark of maturity is the capacity to face reality—problems as well as promises, weaknesses as well as strengths, limitations as well as possibilities.

Buoyed by "You have what it takes; go for it all" and "The sky's the limit" kinds of comments from family members and friends, I threw myself totally into my work, with no thought of an eventual depletion of resources, the need for breathers, the necessity of replenishment, and the long-term negative consequences of such frenetic, nonstop ministry. Sure, I could see in others the tragedy of dishonesty with regard to a recognition of limitations. The marriage of a friend breaks up because he does not recognize the impossibility of being all things to all people without losing the bond of intimacy with his wife. Another friend blows it completely. After trying to do everything perfectly, she slides into an unshakable disappointment and decides to do nothing—literally nothing. A respected role model "burns out," and in a state of total fatigue makes a series of bad decisions. All of that bothers me. But I am different. So I thought!

Mixed signals make muddled thoughts. On the one hand, wise professionals counsel, "Watch out for yourself. Take a day off. Refuse to take on too much." But then implicit suggestions from seminary days speak: "Become the best theologian, the best scriptural exegete, the best preacher, and the best pastoral counselor possible." (Attempting to do one's best in any one of these disciplines involves a lifetime of hard work.) Add to the lingering images of student years the actual expectations in a specific situation (both those formally written in job descriptions and those informally discussed in the congregation): "You are to be pastor, preacher, visitor, staff supervisor, public relations expert, denominational worker, administrator, and teacher as well as model family member, active contributor to the community, and an always available friend."

Thoughts about too much to do and taking time off are repressed temporarily, if not dismissed completely, because of the seductive compliments of a sick kind of hero worship: "You are just what everybody needs." "We are so impressed by the long hours you work." "You always show up at the right moment." "I worry about you, but I think it is wonderful that you don't feel you can take a day off." "You are everything our church wants you to be." "We need you so much." All of that sounds good (especially when self-esteem is sagging). Spurred on by praise, one defies more and more limitations in pursuit of more and more affirmations.

What makes everything worse is the development of a distorted perspective in which attempting the impossible is deemed more religious than doing the possible. Sheer ignorance in one's approach to work is mistakenly lauded as commitment. When physical fatigue develops, emotional imbalance seems near, mental faculties slow down percepti-bly, and stopping seems like the next logical move, thoughts turn to the nineteenth-century cleric who defied good judgment with the rationale, "What is a candle for but to burn?" Yes, that sounds very holy. Full steam ahead on all fronts.

With not-too-heartfelt apologies to the pervasive, cult-building philosophy of the power of positive thinking, I want to declare emphatically that to be able to think something is not—*not!*—to be able to do something. The legitimate joy that comes with a sense of being chosen by God for a certain task or submitting to special training as a part of preparing to serve God in multiple ways is unparalleled. Conversely, the sadness that eventually emerges when one confuses being called to service by God with being commissioned to serve as God is incomparable. Invincibility is not produced by the most profound spirituality. Not even the most exemplary commitment to holiness can eradicate limitations. Discipleship involves obedience within, not without, limitations—regardless of how positive are thoughts to the contrary!

"You could die." How is that for beginning (being required) to face limitations? I was sitting in the office of my medical doctor listening to her describe the possible consequences of my current level of blood pressure. "Either change your lifestyle and take this medication or face the immediate possibility of a stroke or a heart attack," she continued. Not only did my doctor have my undivided attention, she had my hurriedly voiced pledge of cooperation.

When I displayed an obvious concern about this medical situation, some church members encouraged me to make substantive changes in my activities and others instructed me to not think much about it: "A lot of people have high blood pressure. Medication can control it. Don't let the doctor's words frighten you. You still can do pretty much what you want to do." At long last, I knew a setup when I heard it. The voices behind the "Change nothing, don't slow down" words belonged to people as wrong in their expectations of their pastor as in their counsel for him. I was beginning to take seriously important limits related to physical activity.

During the weeks that followed, I received a crash course of comprehensive instruction on limitations—mental, emotional, and spiritual as well as physical. My participation in this experiential curriculum was forced, not chosen. I was an unwilling student. But learning took place.

Confronting emotional limitations was very disconcerting. I took pride in a pastoral sensitivity that made possible identification with persons in diverse emotional situations. How I felt never was an issue. How other people needed me to feel or wanted me to feel was primary. As a result, I practically lost touch with my own emotions.

Most difficult to admit was my lack of a capacity for prolonged emotional honesty. At the very moment I felt filled with fear or folly, anxiety or anger, appreciation or disgust, those around me were not aware that I felt anything at all. To my dismay, I eventually discovered that only in rare instances did I allow anyone ever to see what I was feeling. Not even the people with whom I spent the most time were aware of the emotions present within me.

Following my hospitalization, a doctor told me that much of my struggle in recent years was symptomatic of a search for intimacy. I was shocked. Actually, I thought myself to be better at that than most people. Efforts at a more accurate recognition of my emotions brought me face to face with the reality of limitations—emotional limitations.

Mental limitations seemed easy to overcome. What isn't known, learn! I thought. Though I never have envisioned myself as intellectually smart, I always have committed myself to reading, listening, and studying so as to learn as much as possible. Thus, recognized mental limitations were interpreted as indications of a need for more learning. Given enough information and time for the exercise of reason, I surmised that the worst problems could be readily resolved.

Such an attitude characterized even my approach to

depression. Just after my admission into the hospital, a therapist inquired regarding my thoughts and feelings about my stay there. Immediately I outlined a well-thought-out agenda for discovering answers to certain questions, reasoning through specific difficulties, and achieving specific goals. That therapist kindly told me to toss aside my agenda and to refrain from trying to understand everything. Another doctor was more blunt: "Stop thinking. You think too much already. Your problem is not reason. You can't handle what is unreasonable, the irrational." (Would you believe, I immediately tried to "understand" that diagnosis, to "make sense" of it?)

My resignation from the pastorate was met by a proliferation of rumors. As I began to hear the various "explanations" of my decision, I sought to trace each one to its source. My intention was in reality an illusion—if I could identify each perpetrator of untruths, challenge the dishonesty involved, examine the causes of misunderstanding, and reasonably answer any questions in a clarification of the situation, facts would prevail and destructive stories would be prevented. I tried. And I failed. Rumors, which once started have a life of their own, resist reason. People interested in rumors are uninterested in facts, especially if the rumors make for a more interesting story. Here again, knowledge was of no help.

Admitting an inability to understand, to make sense of, and to explain everything is not yet easy for me. However, I do (still begrudgingly at times) recognize the reality. Many of the most important dimensions of life, good and bad, completely defy reason.

The reality of spiritual limitations got lost under a false sense of competency to meet all pastoral obligations. Others believed in such a provision long before I did. Mistakenly, claims were made that God complements a person's commitment to Christian ministry with an endowment of all kinds of abilities. But, more significantly, attempting to do the impossible was presented as a far more spiritual act than exercising God-given talents in the realm of the practical. Before succumbing to the point of view pressed by peers, my skepticism about this matter was healthy. But eventually I became blind to limitations.

Hurt as well as maturity comes from the important recognition that no person can minister effectively to the spiritual needs of everyone. Some people have problems that I simply do not have the spiritual resources to help solve. At times my own spiritual needs make it necessary for me to elevate receiving ministry from others over doing ministry for others.

Fighting limits is a losing battle. Accepting limits is healthy as well as wise. To ignore, defy, or deny limits is to move from the realm of seeking to serve God into the arena of attempting to play God. God forbid!

REAL DEPRESSION
"YOU ARE SO STRONG AND CONFIDENT."

"How do you sit there so calmly? You are so strong and confident." A middle-aged woman nervously unloading her anxieties about a necessary hospitalization paused to insert that question and observation. All she could see of me was a demeanor of coolness. What I felt inside, however, was far different from the exterior presentation of stability. Stomach muscles knotted. Thoughts raced back and forth between surmise and suspicion, from, Maybe I can help, to, I'm not sure I know what to do or to say. But, if the image I projected reassured this lady, I must have been doing something right, I thought.

"I wish just once you would mess up in a sermon or in another way show us some weakness." The words were spoken by a parishioner as she shook my hand on her way out of a service of worship. I was stunned as I listened. Immediately I acknowledged the strength of the facade behind which I labored. Realizations rushed to the front of my mind: This person has no idea how hard I work to prevent flaws in sermons and to cover up multiple inadequacies. Perhaps I should have said, "Just wait. If you want to see weaknesses in your pastor, you are about to be richly blessed."

Deception was a way of life. But absolutely nothing dishonest, vicious, or harmful was intended. Self-aggrandizement was not even the issue. In my distorted judgment, I was being—doing and saying—what a minister ought to be. Surely a "person of God" would present an image of confident strength. Thus repressing negatives, disguising fatigue, faking happiness, and covering up nervousness or insecurity were instinctive actions, staple ingredients in a way of life that seemed as natural as breathing.

Why? Who said ministers must always be strong? Where are the precedents for perfection among the people of God? Certainly not in the biblical records or the annals of ecclesiastical history.

A diagnosis of depression hit me hard. Now I shudder as I remember the initial thoughts which at the time seemed so important: What will people say? What about my image of strength? Will parishioners lose confidence in me? I must hide this depression until I get over it. No one besides my wife needs to know.

Respect for the doctor prevented an argumentative defensiveness to which I was prone. But questions abounded. Though I had studied depression, I wanted the matter discussed thoroughly. Unfortunately, the doctor's explanation did not square with my hypotheses. Far too much time passed before I ceased attempting to function as physician as well as patient.

Depression did not fit into my scheme of things, personally or professionally. This was not supposed to happen to me. My tendency to intellectualize everything shifted into high gear. I read books and articles about depression. I thought through theories on depression. I remembered ministerial heroes who experienced depression—Harry Emerson Fosdick, Frederick W. Robertson, Phillips Brooks. But none of that mental work helped. Reason was overwhelmed by emotions. I decided the depression still had to be hidden.

Head and heart battled for dominance. The doctor carefully explained that the source of my depression was an internal chemical imbalance aggravated, but not caused by, external factors. My condition required medication. The doctor talked of a disorder; I worried over a weakness. "Chemical imbalance" seemed like a cop-out. "This is a matter of flawed spirituality and insufficient faith," I told myself. "An authentic person of faith never would be in this position." A heavy sense of inferiority prompted embarrassment.

None of my feelings about depression conformed to the carefully reasoned counsel I had offered to others who were depressed: "You have no reason to be ashamed. This is a crisis of health, not faith. You must treat depression as you would treat a bad case of the flu." Such textbook wisdom notwithstanding, disturbed emotions had prevailed.

Finally the time had come when depression could no longer be disguised completely. Others' awareness of my situation led to words intended to help, which in reality inflicted hurt. "I pray that one morning soon you will just wake up and all this depression will be gone. You know it doesn't have to be this way. God can remove depression." ("Then why in heaven's name does God not remove it?" I screamed to myself, fearing a serious failure of my spirit.) "You must make up your mind to feel better. Adopt a more positive attitude. Quit moping around. Get things done." (Such words incited rage and disgust and deepened the depression: I don't even want to get out of bed, much less "get things done." I did not choose to be like this. I feel as helpless in trying to remove the depression by positive thoughts as a cancer patient attempting to excise the malignancy with a good attitude.)

As depression had worsened, I became convinced that no one understood me. Despising self-pity, I sought to shift my primary focus away from myself. The result was a greater preoccupation with my condition. How poorly I felt was all I wanted to talk about around members of my family. But no sooner were words of complaint out of my mouth than I was disgusted that anything at all had been said. Countless times I resolved never again to speak of my feelings. Countless times I broke that resolution. I wanted someone to understand.

For a very long time I had functioned with the depression. Skills in deception still worked effectively enough to prevent parishioners from knowing my true feelings. Ironically, in the midst of some really bad moments light flickered temporarily as the same old kind of adulatory comments set off systems of denial and projected images with no reality—"I so much admire your strength. Your attitude is such an inspiration to us." By then, though, any surge of diversionary pleasure subsided as quickly as it appeared. I no longer believed in myself, even if others did.

Relief—tremendous relief—was experienced when finally I unconditionally admitted my long-term depression and seriously requested more help. At a moment when panic could have prevailed an unexpected peace presided. At last I knew what I should have known all along: I do not have to be strong to qualify as a person of faith. I do not have to keep going for the sake of perpetuating a responsible ministerial image. I can determine to find help for myself and to take care of myself without succumbing to rank selfishness. Finally!

Ministers can be depressed. When that is the case, help is needed. The responses, therapy, and recuperation required for clergy persons are no different from those which are essential to all depressed people.

INSATIABLE AMBITION
"YOU WORK SO HARD AND DO SO MUCH GOOD."

Raw ambition disguised as religious devotion is a terror to behold. Unfortunately, the similarity between their appearances and the ability of feelings to play tricks with motivations make a neat separation of the two most difficult. No one is exempt from possible self-deception. Drivenness can look just like holiness, even when the two are totally unrelated.

Long hours of hard work seemed consistent with my early spiritual commitment. Opportunities for education and ministry were viewed as divine gifts to be accepted gladly and responsibly. Sensing my accountability to God for a good stewardship of time and talents, I intended to claim every possibility for service and to use every moment to the fullest. At the time, I was all right. I also valued rest, serendipitous excursions, and fun. At that point, life had about it the rhythm of creation. Time was allocated appropriately between "hitting it hard" and "backing off." My lifestyle was more than defensible—it was commendable and healthy.

Healthy people can get sick. Goals are redefined almost imperceptibly. Admirable attributes deteriorate into deplorable liabilities. Success becomes more important than service. Demonstrating productivity is a higher priority than maintaining a healthy personality (after all, that can be faked if necessary). Character traits and behavioral patterns that once looked good and were good continue to look good, though they have gone bad. I got sick.

What happens? I have no expertise to answer that question generally. I only have some sense of what happened to me personally. Several factors were involved.

Insecurity was an issue—a wide range of insecurities, actually. Internal arguments were seldom quieted: I have the credentials and the competence to do this job. Yes, but I'm not as good as I'm supposed to be. Preaching is my strong suit. Why, then, do some people not like my preaching? Maybe I'm not continuing to grow in this area of ministry. Evidently people come to me for counsel because they find help. What, though, if I am saying the wrong things, offering bad advice? Eventually other insecurities also demanded attention—financial and relational, for example.

Increased activity was my response to insecurity—work harder on preaching, read more in depth in specific areas of counseling, make more visits, accept more invitations that promise financial remuneration, develop new friendships. I wanted to project an appearance of security even if I could not feel it internally.

Then, too, I like to be liked. Pleasing other people always has been pleasurable for me. A dominant assumption was that everyone likes a person who does everything well professionally and still knows how to anticipate the need of a neighbor and when to place a call to a friend. That assumption (move over, God) gave me direction. Now at times I wonder if I made impressive numbers of hospital visits because of genuine care, a desire to please the patients, a hope for affirmation from the congregation, or a mixture of all of that, projected as ministry. In relation to counselees, I must ask if I spoke the right words because they were right and I believed them or because they were the statements the persons wanted to hear. Were the constant cross-country treks by plane indicative of my desire to serve or to impress? Was I trying to be responsible or recognizable? Perhaps the most serious of all of the retrospective inquiries centers on the issue of whether I was living or just performing.

To be sure, motives are rarely, if ever, pure. Multiple motivations undergird almost all of people's actions. Few are the folks who, at one time or another, have not done the right thing for the wrong reason.

Success was as much the object of my infatuation as the subject of my criticism. To speak of success in relation to ministry was unthinkable. (Ministerial conversations often are filled with double-talk. Fierce competition between ministers is real but unmentionable. Standards for measuring achievement come straight from the statistically oriented world of business. But that admission is avoided, and talk adroitly steers clear of references to such a crass concept of success. Frequently, references to accomplishments and boasts about achievements are conveyed only in terms such as "sacrifices," "victories for the Lord," or "blessings"—all of which are countable.) So in my thoughts I equated service with success and went after it at a sprintlike pace, while in my words I condemned success-minded persons and exalted service. I had the best of both worlds—the more I "served," the more "success" I achieved. Notations of all my work to advance God's reign ultimately would end up as line items on my résumé.

Given such mental calisthenics sustained by emotional strength, productivity became an obsession. A full calendar was indicative of a fulfilling life. I wrote articles while on plane trips to deliver speeches. While preaching at one meeting, I set in motion plans to do the same thing somewhere else. As I took on more assignments in the community, I increased the number of hours I devoted to counseling. One morning, in the midst of seeking to finish two manuscripts already contracted for publication, I mailed two proposals for additional publication projects.

"I don't see how you get so much done." "Everywhere I turn, I meet someone who recently has heard you speak or just read something new you have written." "I hope you know that your long hours of work yield untold amounts of good." Such comments constituted music to my ears, a solace for my soul. Or so I thought. Actually, the words were more akin to gasoline tossed onto a raging fire.

Doing—accomplishing, achieving—may have become an escape from being. Such a procedure is relatively easy to bring off in the ministry (and one even can look good doing it). Facing up to personal or family needs can be avoided by making another pastoral call (one more is always on the list). Reflection on the substance of one's existence can be pushed aside for the composition of one more homily. Spending time on someone else's spirituality is a legitimate substitute for giving attention to one's own spirituality. Few will challenge a preoccupation with action. To the contrary, many will praise it.

How much is enough? If a satisfactory answer to that question ever took shape in my head, it did not make it to my heart. Given a flawed human ambition understood as a commission from God and lauded by the affirmations of well-meaning associates, I knew no such thing as enough. I always was ready to serve on another board, to schedule one more engagement, to accept an additional writing assignment.

Fulfillment (or the lack of it) also was a crucial issue. By my late thirties I had achieved most of the professional goals established in my twenties. I had taught in both college and seminary classrooms, worked in Christian social ethics for the denominational agency I respected most, traveled extensively, written curriculum materials as well as numerous articles for denominational-based publications, preached on national television, published several books, visited with many of my heroes, and served on strategic boards (civil and religious). I was pastoring the kind of church I had dreamed of pastoring. Everything looked great. But it wasn't. I was plagued not by the question of what to do next, but by the realization of incompleteness at the moment. Living on the edge was common. Surely there is something more—one more book, one more interview, one more recognition—that will produce a lasting sense of fulfillment, I thought. Ambition was now aimed at satisfaction.

But I looked in the wrong places. Resolutions were made to work harder and be more productive. My actions made as much sense as a dieter overeating in order to lose weight.

Driving ambition does not die easily. Just days ago, in a telephone conversation with a friend I had not seen for years, my friend inquired about my health. Quickly I changed the subject from how I was feeling to what I had been doing. I wanted my friend to know of my productivity. Wisely, she interrupted me to point out that many matters are more important than productivity and it would be just fine if I would enjoy some time with no concern for production. (She did not know she was speaking to a man who carried a packed briefcase to the hospital with every intention of using that respite to get a lot of work done.)

Obviously, I do not have this problem licked. But finally I have heard someone say of doing nothing, "That's good," and I have received affirmation for a lack of production. Maybe I can allow these compliments to encourage my continued movement toward health in the same way I allowed high praises for my constant work to enable me to move toward sickness, and judge it as another accomplishment on the way to success.

AN INADEQUATE THEOLOGY
"YOU HAVE SUCH A REMARKABLE FAITH."

Introducing his classic work *A Theology of the Social Gospel,* Walter Rauschenbusch observed that most often experience precedes theology. In every age, major theological ideas were shaped in response to actual situations. Not so with me. My theology developed outside the crucible of comprehensive human experience (almost as if in a sterile laboratory). Perhaps that was the reason for its inadequacy.

Some theology I knew only with my head. Other theology I embraced with my head and my heart. The latter was as sufficient as the former was inadequate.

My earliest helpings of theology were served up by respected theologians with successful careers. Though life was not easy then, it was happy. I studied in institutions I loved. Good friends were all around. Extracurricular involvements varied between satisfaction and fun. Ministry was proceeding in the direction desired. Naturally, setbacks and disappointments occurred. But negatives did not prevail.

I discovered scholarly elaborations that confirmed such prior convictions as the sufficiency of belief and the priority of prayer. Though I resented the cliché "Everything will be all right," that was the fundamental assumption by which I functioned. Confident that problems required only delays or temporary detours, never a permanent rerouting of life, I proceeded to build a theology suitable for the good times, but problematic because it was untested by bad times.

Hurt's pervasiveness and the omnipresence of difficulties in people's lives did not escape me. I knew the identity of Jesus as a suffering servant among his disciples, the centrality of the cross in the New Testament, and the necessity of struggle in the lives of pilgrims. But my knowledge was mostly academic. I had not lived what I thought. I spoke of difficulties without knowing defeat and addressed failures from a perspective of success. While I talked a lot about hurt and sought to help troubled people, I was functioning as a trained minister, not as an experienced person who ministers.

My theology was full of neat explanations for tough questions. A "biblically based" reason could be cited for even the most bewildering situations. This "answer man" identity brought praise and compliments—"You have such a remarkable faith." I was big on not-to-be-questioned ultimatums heralded by "Thus says the Lord." Imperatives outnumbered indicatives. Calls to duty took precedence over promises of mercy. Judgment was a more fruitful topic for consideration than grace. I had much more to say to persons inflicting hurt than to individuals experiencing hurt.

When hurt happened and pain struck in my life, I scurried back to the theological drawing board. More work had to be done. My problem was not untruths, but half-truths or incomplete truths. I had confused a glimpse at a partial insight with a perception of the total.

At long last I was beginning to understand another whole dimension of theology. And my comprehension was experiential as well as intellectual. Authentic love and suffering appear inseparable. God's grace is as debatable as it is inevitable. Forgiveness is as costly as are the sins that make it necessary. Difficulties can be occasions for deepening faith. But none of this came easily. Struggle had become a synonym for living.

Then things got worse. I knew love involved suffering, but I thought such suffering would be rewarded. Not so. I surmised that faith born in conflict would be praised (not criticized). I imagined that people who affirmed messages on grace were committed to live by grace. Wrong. I viewed forgiveness as an avenue to humans' involvement in divine restoration, rather than as a cultural buzzword to be sounded while finishing off someone standing in the way of perfection. No.

Undoubtedly my developing depression aggravated the theological problem. For the first time I was confronting problems for which I could see no good solutions. I had to deal with situations in which I knew everything would *not* turn out all right.

Soon everything seemed up for grabs. The very beliefs that became most important to me amid the hurt appeared to cause more hurt. After rereading with profound appreciation and identifying with Henri Nouwen's *The Wounded Healer*, I concluded that his concept was not for ministers in the churches I knew. Congregations familiar to me wanted healers, but no wounds, please. Feeling rejection at the very time I sensed my potential for effective ministry was greater than ever, I realized that most of the experiences that a Nouwen would see as credentials for ministry are viewed by others as intolerable liabilities.

"Your problem was people, not theology," someone could charge. Perhaps. However, if people refuse to embrace basic beliefs or, more likely, if people affirm biblical fundamentals in theory but resort to other principles in practice, does that not raise important questions about the viability of the theology as well as the integrity of the people? Human weaknesses I understand. Confessing the reality of evil is not difficult. The people dimension of the matter is not a problem. Bothering me, though, was the suspicion that doctrine is not powerful enough to affect action. Yes, I believe in the rightness of grace, forgiveness, love, and reconciliation, but I question whether they really work (or whether or not they will be given a chance to work). Can the realities of the gospel ever become personal? Or is the power of the gospel inept in relation to cultural pulls and human wills? Maybe one cannot actually live by the gospel now—in church or in society. (Nietzsche said the last Christian died on the cross.)

Most dangerous was the attraction of painless peace— actually an impossibility apart from death. Hurt had lasted long enough and depression deepened to such an extent that popular theological declarations guaranteed to evoke praise were enticing. Convictions caused me problems. I watched and listened as others laid out theological platitudes that attracted large crowds of people supportive of the "theology" and devoted to the "theologian." Why not? I thought. Personally, I don't agree. But what do I know? My beliefs just seem to cause trouble. An irrational hunger for affirmation threatened to override biblical truth in setting my theological direction.

Many times persons who heard one of my sermons or counselees who aspired to what they saw as the level of my belief commented, "You have such a strong faith." Hearing, I have sensed a shuffle in my soul, felt a twinge within my conscience, and said to myself, "How I wish you were right! But little do you know." My pursuit of an adequate theology seems to require a relentless uphill climb.

Perception is not reality; powerful, yes, but not reality. Maybe I preferred perception for so long because the outcome was positive—I looked better than I was, better than anyone can be. When the tables turned, so that perception worked against me rather than for me, I changed, placing a premium on reality.

When a false perception prevails over the truth of a situation, some degree of destruction is inevitable. Showered with unfounded affirmations, a person fails to take himself seriously and thus lives with a self-deception that will crack and then crumble in crises. Conversely, a person who is made the brunt of mistaken criticisms and misinformed condemnations may be prevented from achieving her God-given potential. Both situations qualify as tragedy.

Though my motivation to deal with reality was not exemplary, the result was healthy. Misperceptions, positive and negative, continue to present major problems. But I want no part of them, whether I am glorified or victimized by the identity at stake.

My story does not exist in isolation. Christian ministry and ministers are in need of demythologization (I have wanted to use that word in a published sentence ever since I first heard it in a seminary classroom). Jesus is the only Messiah. None of the rest of us can come close. A call to serve God is radically different from a summons to serve as God.

Persons in the ministry represent a cross section of humanity. A potential for evil (morally speaking) and failure (professionally speaking) is just as real as a potential for admirable righteousness or great success. The realization of either is no reason for adulation or condemnation. Things change quickly. A human being is still involved. Besides, the ultimate judgment upon a ministry and the final determination about the usefulness of a minister belong only to God.

Every minister needs a minister. Demands for total competency can become heavy. Divine causes can get very sick. Pure meanness can be perpretrated under a guise of righteousness. Meeting behind a sign that reads "church" does not guarantee the people involved will act like church. Help from beyond oneself is essential for the maintenance of sanity and strength, not to mention a proper spiritual perspective and healthy personhood. A minister can victimize others. A minister can be victimized by others. Every minister needs a minister.

Wise ministers daily pray to God and faithfully take care of themselves. At times an opportunity for service qualifies as a challenge and justifies an unrestricted expenditure of one's best efforts. At other times, contemporary ministers do well to emulate the actions of their predecessors who in obedience to their Lord departed from situations, dramatically shaking from their sandals every lingering particle of dust from the site.

The human destruction of deception has divine motivation. Exploding myths and facing facts is holy work (and, not surprisingly, the labor of human beings desirous of good health).

2
"Honest Confession Is Good for the Soul"

Smacking her lips humorously while looking very serious, my high school English teacher barked like a Marine drill instructor, "Honest confession is good for the soul." Why did those words always make students want to scoot down behind our desks with feelings of guilt even if we had no reasons for guilt? Frankly, I do not remember a great deal more of Miss Mary Sue Dunn's specific contributions to my adolescent years of education, but I have never forgotten her reiterated assertion. Her words of wisdom were battered into students' consciences at least three or four times daily. *Honest confession is good for the soul.*

Though I have remembered these words from this early mentor, I must admit (in their spirit) that I have not always agreed with them. Except for the qualification that follows, suffice it to point out that I have not always found confession to be a *good* experience. Certainly I am well aware of biblical admonitions in which readers are advised to practice confession as a prerequisite to receiving forgiveness. However, Jesus seemed to challenge the *quid pro quo* attitude, the mechanical, almost magical, ritual, implied by such passages when he extended the offer of forgiveness to people who neither requested it nor confessed a reason to request it. But that is material for another book. Honest confession is good for the soul? Maybe. Maybe not.

Before anyone scornfully assails me with charges of being "soft on dishonesty," I hasten to affirm that confession—yes, Miss Dunn, honest confession—*is* necessary if a negative experience is eventually to be viewed positively, to be interpreted as a step toward greater personal maturity. Honest confrontations with reality are essential for all people who desire a better future, a future devoid of both the symptoms of the problems and the actual problems of the past. Reality is important here too. Honest confession is not easy, may not always be a contributor to immediate peace, will not by itself alter errors, and cannot take the place of corrective action. But good? Yes, honest confession is good. So, here goes.

If depression is a raging river which after overflowing its natural boundaries sweeps destructively across all in its path, flooding, smothering, and thus threatening life itself, improved conditions are possible only as the several tributaries emptying into the depths of the disturbance and swelling its turbulence are identified and brought under control. Depression is a problem. But depression is also the result of, and thus symptomatic of, other problems. The devastating waters of an out-of-control flooding river cannot be expected to recede until the problematic streams that flow into that river return to normal. Depression itself cannot be resolved satisfactorily until all the surging systems contributing to it are addressed helpfully.

Honest confession about depression involves far more than the admission, "I am depressed." Usually that statement is not made without considerable difficulty. Personally, I had big problems just saying those words. But equally as difficult, if not more so, and equally essential for movement toward improved health, are an identification and understanding of those sources of emotions which have erupted individually, but over time have converged to form and to sustain depression.

"YOU ARE DEPRESSED!"

"You are depressed and have been for four or five years." The words were spoken to me in 1982 by my longtime, much-respected, absolutely trusted friend Wayne Oates. No casual observation, the opinion was a professional one offered on the basis of his renowned expertise. Though I did not doubt Wayne's assessment, I did not understand him, not really. I knew I was facing major problems which dominated my thoughts and drained my emotions. But my self-diagnosis would have focused on stress, worry, disappointment, fatigue, and sadness. Not depression. That word sounded weak, unrespectably sick, like an embarrassing character flaw. (Long ago, in a seminary classroom, Wayne Oates introduced me to the old axiom: "He who has himself for a doctor has a fool for a patient." Now, years later, this beloved professor illustrated the wisdom of his remark with a personal application of its truth to me.)

Depression sounded like a logical description of my situation. However, I seriously questioned the accuracy of labeling it long-term. I did agree to begin taking some medication, a small daily dosage of a mild antidepressant. Taking medicine for a problem tends to legitimize it as a "real" illness, whatever its nature.

Soon a major move was made—geographical relocation and a different professional assignment—which presented new opportunities for ministry, new challenges to stir my creative juices, and new friends with whom to form covenants evidenced in giving and receiving. A radically different setting in which to live offered the encouraging promise of obviously welcome possibilities. But an internal nagging of old problems, recognized by me if by no one else, raised the specter that life-enhancing activities fraught with significant meaning might go unclaimed because of my failure to deal decisively with sources of depression. Diverse streams swept with swirling currents which assured a continuation of rough waters at dangerous depths. How could another flood be avoided?

Not only can I fool other people rather convincingly most of the time, I can fool myself some of the time. Involvement in a university-based ministry dictated a radically altered daily itinerary from that required by a parish pastorate. Demands were diminished and freedom heightened. Quickly I took on a heavy load of writing assignments, speaking engagements, and other extracurricular activities in addition to my primary responsibilities. Having so much to do seemed extremely good for my ego, even if not for my health. But, who knows, I thought, time will take care of everything.

Surprise, surprise. No. Absolutely not. I knew the truth. I had declared it in sermons and discussed it with counselees. Internal difficulties move with a person and refuse to be erased by changed surroundings or replaced by busyness, whatever its importance. Needless to say, after several months I had to take seriously once again that not all was right inside (maybe nothing was right inside).

When I spoke with a professional about my difficulties, he diagnosed a mild depression, prescribed a weak drug, and suggested periodic consultations. For the next six months I took my medication, talked with the doctor intermittently, and tried to hang on to an emotional roller coaster that seemed to creep along a flat, boring expanse of space for a time and then suddenly plummet to an indescribable bottom, leaving me washed out and listless. Occasionally a slow climb to a higher emotional level occurred. Generally, though, I stayed in the depths for so long that I tended to forget life could go any higher.

Anger developed toward my doctor. Our visits produced a predictable pattern. After entering the doctor's office and exchanging greetings with him, I sat down on his couch and waited for some indication of what was to come next. Silence ruled the room until I spoke. What I said in those opening moments usually determined the direction of our conversation for the remainder of the hour. I resented that.

For one thing, I was adept enough at masking emotions to look and sound fine even when I was in terrible shape. I knew the right words to speak and actions to discuss in order to demonstrate improvement and to document health. I wanted the doctor to call my bluff if necessary to draw from me the sickening depression as a dentist would extract a throbbing tooth with irreversible decay. Though weary with the costly charade, I was too stubbornly private and too well trained in cover-ups to come clean about my condition.

A second reason for my resentment toward the doctor related to his passivity and lack of specificity in counsel. Memory took me back to a much earlier visit to a school-sponsored medical clinic. After the doctor for the day asked me what was wrong and I described my sore throat, the physician declared authoritatively, "You have a sore throat." I paid to come here for that! I thought.

Actually, the doctor with whom I was consulting excelled in diagnosis but not in long-term helpfulness. I thoroughly enjoyed his careful analysis of my self-defined situation and the extended dialogues that developed as together we retraced those routes which I had traveled in the past in order to arrive at the present. But, diagnosis and analysis alone do little to improve an illness.

Finally, one day I pulled together enough determination to level with my doctor about the major discrepancies that existed between my life as discussed in his office and my life as experienced in attempting to get through most other days. Maybe that is what he had been waiting for. Immediately he launched into a long series of questions, studied each of my answers, and then said, "You are clinically depressed." I wanted to shout, "Hurrah!" Though I did not know exactly what it meant to be "clinically depressed," I felt great relief, thinking, At least an explanation exists for why I feel this way. Now, maybe something can be done about getting better. The diagnosis was by far the worst yet. But I felt better about my situation than I had in months.

I remained on medication for clinical depression for over three years. From time to time, the doctor changed the type of drug taken and altered the dosages prescribed. At one point, I was allowed to drop the use of one prescription. On several occasions I requested the implementation of a plan aimed at the abandonment of all medications. Each time, however, the doctor preferred a "continue-as-is, wait-and-see" response. I trusted him and continued to follow his directions.

Most obvious as a weakness in the scenario of my treatment was the infrequency of my sessions with the doctor. I take full responsibility for this. Scheduling appointments was left to my discretion, with no professional direction. Sessions were expensive and, in my opinion, nonproductive. So I did not request consultations until times when I felt I could not continue as things were.

A memory from childhood emerged in relation to the pattern of my treatments. After I complained of a toothache or a stomachache, my parents made an appointment with a physician and rushed me to the clinic. Then, while sitting in the doctor's waiting room, I realized the pain was gone and I was feeling fine. Several times that same sensation was experienced after arriving for a consultation. Perhaps I tried to substitute going to the doctor or talking to the doctor for listening to the doctor's advice and setting myself on a course of treatment to improve my health. Obviously, I made a serious error.

Evident to the reader by now is the fact that for several years I barely acknowledged the presence of depression in my life, much less attempted to deal with it—ignoring it when I could and never admitting it to anyone else. Of course, sources of the depression were not addressed at all. Another change in my professional position once again created new circumstances, which delayed still longer the much overdue, always essential honest confession—the prelude necessary to receiving help.

Complicating my problem and delaying my request for significant help in dealing with it were the mixed signals within my personality and ministry. Panic and hurt inside did not completely stifle good conversations, smiles, and laughter. Sliding downward into new depths of sorrow evidenced in tears and ascending to wonderful heights of happiness bordering on hilarity were interpreted as indications of a maturing capacity for greater sensitivity. In some moments, I knew better. But seldom, if ever, was I able to say what I knew.

While I was sinking deeper and deeper into depression, I was performing some ministerial tasks better and better. Both family members and friends were telling me that my preaching, in terms of both sermon content and public delivery, was the best it ever had been. I agreed, knowing that the primary explanation for this development centered on the subjects of my sermons. My pulpit work was speaking perceptively and powerfully to people's struggles because I was engaged in such a terrible struggle within myself. Sermons that spoke to people's most profound hurts were personally experiential as well as thoroughly biblical.

Though I was aware that my preaching ministry was going well, I knew that never before had I found less satisfaction in it. When I sat down to write a sermon, thoughts flowed. However, my carefully developed discipline related to sermon development had deteriorated. Also gone was the old all-day-Saturday and early-Sunday-morning eagerness to preach. In its place was dread, fed by the thought, I don't believe I can do it today. Amazingly, the preaching event went well. But the result in me was total depletion.

Not all phases of my ministry escaped the negative consequences of depression. A longtime commitment to careful and consistent administration became virtually nonexistent. Pieces of correspondence that should have been answered the day after they were received lay on my desk unattended for weeks. (One particular letter stands out in my mind. Each time I looked at it I knew the need for an immediate response. Even that realization did not move me to action.) Committee work was left undone. Some pastoral phone calls were not made.

Despite those realities, if anyone had walked into my office and said, "You are not functioning well. You are depressed. You need help," I would have argued vehemently. Undoubtedly, I would have handed over an article just completed for a scholarly journal and a chapter I had prepared for inclusion in a soon-to-be-published *festschrift* to honor a friend. I would have cited successes in recent counseling sessions and positive reactions during visits with prospective church members.

In retrospect, I do not know what I would have believed had I heard such a comment that I was suffering an illness. Even if I had known the person offering the assessment was right, I do not know that I would have admitted it. That is the curse. Just enough of life was going well to argue convincingly (with myself as well as with others), "I'm all right." But much more was wrong than was right.

Eventually the moment of truth came. It always does. Depression does not just suddenly vanish when it fails to receive attention. I learned that the hard way.

Dealing with a serious, potentially explosive problem in the church and receiving the medical diagnosis of a severe, potentially life-threatening level of hypertension combined to produce the decision for hospitalization. Reluctantly, I consented. Underneath the anxiety, worry, fear, embarrassment, anger, and discomfort associated with being admitted to the hospital, buried so deeply as to be mostly unnoticeable, I did feel a faint stirring of hope.

Once in a clinical setting, confessing depression was easy. All around me were people for whom depression seemed of little more consequence than an occasional sneeze in a cancer patient's day, given the severity of emotional disorders plaguing them. That environment did not cause me to lose sight of the critical nature of my problem, however, or to experience great ecstasy on hearing an honest appraisal of the sources of my depression.

No one act of clinical care was decisive in the improvement of my health. Rather, a combination of factors—a climate that encouraged honest thoughts and words; the presence of sensitive, supportive therapists; a helpful reassessment of the complex nature of depression; and an emerging desire, if not an absolute commitment, to getting better—prodded me to deal comprehensively with my dilemma. With more patience than I generally can muster, I gave myself to looking at and thinking about how I got to this particular time in my life.

Here are notations about some of the significant tributaries that fed the depression which flooded my life. At moments I had hopes of a recession of the overwhelming turbulence, a cessation of the devastation, and a recovery of life as normal. Floods do subside. At other moments, though, I considered the possibility that I had seriously misread the situation which, in reality, included a broadside by an emotional tidal wave, the very destructive force of which would make thoughts of a recoverable future more the product of a Pollyannaish fantasy than the evidences of a spiritual hope.

These phenomena are separated here for purposes of discussion. In life, no such neat division is possible. My experience of depression involved a mixture of them all at the same time—to such an extent, in fact, that the true identity of any one emotion alone resisted recognition.

STRESS

"I'VE HAD IT! I CAN'T GO ON."

Prolonged involvement in high-tension, especially conflict-laden, circumstances is dangerous. But, typically, the source of problematic stress resides more in what is going on inside a person than in what is taking place around a person. Crucial in managing stress is adaptability. Deterioration in a person's ability to adjust to troublesome situations can contribute to depression. Reciprocally, a person's normal capabilities for healthy reactions to stressful situations can be weakened severely, if not deadened completely, by depression. In unusually difficult situations, a depressed person even may decide to give up or, devoid altogether of decisive thoughts and feelings, just give up.

Until recent years I viewed stress more positively than negatively. I enjoyed being busy, very busy. Some of my best work has been done under pressure. Great fulfillment was derived from meeting short deadlines, from representing a stabilizing perspective amid worsening conditions that threaten to become chaotic, from facilitating conflict resolution, and from walking with people through crisis situations.

My point of view regarding stress changed slowly, almost imperceptibly, but significantly. A major change was predictable. The right-hand side of an equation is "trouble" if the formula on the left-hand side is composed of "seven days a week of work plus unrealistic expectations plus minimal fulfillment."

When I became the senior minister of a large congregation in Texas, I had something to prove. My immediate predecessor in that position was a longtime friend and confidant. After a relatively brief period of ministry there, he resigned from that congregation of five thousand members to accept the pastorate of a church of five hundred members in another state. Subsequently, both in public-speaking engagements and in published writings, my friend reflected on the burden and fatigue associated with ministry in the Texas congregation. Numerous friends shared observations about the heaviness shouldered by the previous pastor and warned me against a similar plight. Confident of my wisdom and strength (after all, I was thirty-five years old), I shrugged off every precaution and assured myself and others that such worry was unnecessary for me. Quietly I resolved to show "them" all that this job could be done without any adverse side effects, physically and emotionally.

For a considerable stretch of time my fantasy of ministerial invincibility remained intact. Routine tasks were fast-paced but enjoyable. Special problems, almost daily, were handled as welcome challenges. More and more responsibilities were accepted. Already long days of work became even longer. Change, significant changes, began.

Diversity, so much a part of the beauty of that congregation, played havoc with administration. Virtually no action enjoyed unanimous support. Criticism from some corner was constant—both destructive and constructive, mean and well-intended. Relational disappointments furthered a growing dis-ease. Rejection from anyone, a given in ministry, was extremely unsettling, since I wanted to be liked by everyone. Emotional emptiness developed, along with physical fatigue.

But I kept up a good front. In fact, I renewed my efforts, intended for public observation, to appear on top of everything. Differences would not be allowed to get me down. I bragged about diversity within the church and encouraged it, though much of the time I despised it. I decided to show my critics how much I was appreciated by others (as if they cared). So I accepted virtually every invitation I received for preaching, lecturing, and writing. Needing rest, I worked harder.

The reader should understand that members of that congregation are not to be blamed for my difficulties. Among the pastoral privileges granted to me by that church were one day a week off, which I rarely took, monthly times away for planning and rest, which I mostly ignored, and even a periodic study leave, which I requested when I became the pastor and then later refused to take because of illusions about the indispensability of the pastor's presence. I am responsible for those decisions and their destructive consequences.

Few, if any, churches will insist that provisions for study and rest be claimed by the pastor. Someone is always in need of pastoral attention. Constantly some question awaits an answer from the pastor. However, a congregation generally will support its pastor when requirements for rest and relaxation are met. If not, all the more reason exists for the pastor to guarantee occasions for retreat and refortification.

In my experience, the absence of fulfillment personally, far more than the presence of a full schedule of ministries, was the essential factor in a submission to stress and the development of depression. One Saturday I did three funerals with grave-side services, provided worship leadership for a wedding ceremony, and attended a dinner with several church members, and still felt fine late that evening, ready for Sunday morning. When the joy left, though, and fulfillment was gone, even the simplest schedules and most routine days were difficult to negotiate. Then, too, I still had to keep up that front of strength. ("Heaven knows, we can't have a weak pastor.") Attempting day after day to mask hurt, cover fatigue, and convince everyone that all is well when all is not well is the most unbearable stress of all.

Moving from that Texas pastorate neither removed my sense of stress nor dispelled my depression. Geographical change alone is devoid of such power. In my next two positions, first in a university and more recently in another local church, my duties were reduced and the potential for time off increased dramatically. Expectations related to my position were much lower than those I had known previously. The numbers of people to be served were much smaller. Assignments were not burdensome. Yet stress continued and depression worsened.

My way of compensating for a less-demanding ministry was to repeat the prior pattern—accept every invitation for preaching and every assignment for writing, work long hours, find meetings to attend, and schedule conferences to lead if an imposed agenda is not readily available. Obviously, the problem was within me, not around me. I left the pastorate in Texas with unfinished business that would not go away without attention, regardless of where I lived and how I ministered.

Most likely, seven years of misery, pain, confusion, and depression could have been avoided had I taken only one year, more or less, sought help, and seriously addressed my problems. But, wait. That does not mean the last seven years have been completely devoid of any pleasure, meaning, accomplishments, and satisfaction. Wonderful experiences have been enjoyed. In reality, though, the good times complicated my problem. Just enough positives existed to justify the negatives' being ignored or repressed.

Once or twice, during really bad times, I found the courage to be honest about my hurts and even to suggest a possible need for hospitalization. Those who listened dismissed my comments with observations about how colleagues envied my position and with statements to the effect that "You just don't realize how good you've got it." Their words were in order. A lot of positive work had been done. Besides, I had continued to develop my expertise in deception. By now I could laugh while wanting to cry, speak when desperately desiring silence, and relate to others while wishing to run for solitude. My cover-up had worked so well that a revelation of my real condition looked like no more than the indication of a bad day.

Most memorable among the sensations when I finally did become hospitalized was an almost immediate reduction in stress. For the first time in years, weariness seemed correctable, rest available.

GUILT
"How can I be so wrong?"

If graduate degrees in guilt were granted for personal experiences, my dossier would document impressive amounts of advanced work in the field beyond a terminal degree bestowed with highest honors. My acquaintance with guilt antedated adulthood and even adolescence, however. I knew the feelings of guilt intimately long before I could give them the correct name. A capacity for guilt developed before the ability to read and write. With the passing of time, though, I became even more adept at shouldering guilt. Both church and home were important centers of education for training in this emotion.

In the environment of my earliest memories the primary motivation for doing good was to avoid doing bad. Terrible consequences were cited as the basic reason for avoiding evil actions. Advice droned over a pointed finger abounded: "You will ruin your health." "People will talk about you." "You will disappoint and hurt your family, who love you." "God will punish you." (The very earliest precedents of these more serious warnings included: "Santa Claus will not come to see you," and "You'd better be careful or your Christmas stocking will be full of switches." Tough stuff for any child!)

Such an indoctrination to morality produced a preoccupation with not doing bad. Every dimension of life was involved—everything from obedience in taking an afternoon nap to refraining from the use of "ugly words," from going to church on Wednesday nights to refusing to play ball on Sunday afternoons. An obsession with the avoidance of guilt nurtures a creative moral casuistry even among the very young. Impressive skills in cutting corners develop quickly. With great dedication, examinations of various actions detail what can be done without doing bad and how close one can come to doing bad without actually being guilty of it.

Whether control by guilt was intended within my family or not, I do not know. But it was there and it worked. That I do know. Often my behavior was motivated not so much by a desire to do the right thing as by a passion to avoid doing the wrong thing and feeling guilty about it. In almost every

instance where wrong had been done, and there were plenty
of such instances, I preferred a tough tongue-lashing or a
hand-spanking from my parents to hurtful words which
inflicted great guilt. Perhaps the only thing worse than
reflections loaded with guilt were up-front injections of
suspicion, advance warnings in the form of those discomforting words that prompted incessant questioning: "Have a
good time, but remember who you are." "Enjoy being with
your friends, but watch your actions." Pleasure was compro-
mised by constant self-interrogation: Did I say the wrong
thing? Is this activity all right or should I avoid it just to be
safe? Should I have refused to laugh at that funny story?
Guilt became such a familiar phenomenon that an absence
of guilt for any extended period of time created guilt.

While there is a question whether guilt was a considered
strategy for discipline and a pedagogical tool for growth in
my home, no doubt exists about the intentional use of guilt
in my church. An obedient faith majored in negatives.
Salvation was understood much more as an escape from hell
than as a means to enjoy the abundance of a life reconciled
with God. Not hating people took precedence over loving
people, because hatred reaps damnation. What happened in
church mattered little as long as one did not miss church.
Guilt was a hook used to snatch persons away from the
enticements and entrapments of evil.

Guilt-wielding legalists breed a ridiculously meticulous
legalism. Every moralism declared becomes the object of
careful study in an effort to negotiate satisfactorily with
guilt. Dancing was wrong. The preacher had stated that fact
repeatedly. But petting with a date was acceptable. Not a
word against that had been spoken. Playing cards was sinful,
especially if the players possessed the kind of cards dealt in
poker. Everybody around me knew that. (Incidentally, playing Old Maid was approved with hesitation. But not Rook.
Both could lead to something worse.) Prejudice, though, was
all right. Why, even Scripture verses could be quoted in
support of judging people who were different as inferior.

When I was about eight years old, to the dismay of members of my family and church, a "beer joint" opened directly across the street from our house. Everybody was indignant. Hasty action seemed appropriate. As a card-carrying member of the young people's division of the local temperance league, I had been taught that even a close proximity to liquor can lead to wrongdoing. In my opinion, that drinking establishment should have had the words "SINNERS" or "GUILTY" printed in large letters (red, of course) across its door. No limits were set, however, in determining appropriate responses to such outcroppings of evil. On that subject the church had been silent. So one afternoon, after enlisting the support of a friend, with a white-hot righteousness accompanied by its appropriate vindictiveness toward all evil, I marched in front of that new neighborhood establishment and hurled rocks at its door, windows, and walls—completely devoid of any feeling of guilt.

Oh, how pleased the Pharisees would be! Doing wrong does not seem to matter much if it is intended to judge, restrict, or punish another wrong.

Similar moral gymnastics (inconsistencies, actually) occur among adults. Actions aimed at avoiding guilt can be instrumental in causing one to do wrong. With great clarity I had understood the biblical injunction to honor parents, and with great intensity I had sought to obey it. However, I did not hear as well and heed as carefully another divine commandment equally important in nature—"a man shall leave his father and mother and be joined to his wife" (Matt. 19:5; see also Gen. 2:24). Not much was said about that in my church. So for far too long attempts to avoid the guilt produced by disobeying the "honor" commandment weakened a proper, biblically affirmed clinging to my wife. I tried so hard to do right in one area that I did wrong in another. Guilt from one direction or the other seemed unavoidable.

Constantly I am amazed by evidences of the lingering strength of childhood guilt in the lives of apparently mature adults (it takes one to know one). Mental tapes produced early in life continue to be played by respected authority figures as potent influences in the feelings, decisions, and actions of their later lives. Breakthroughs in practical wisdom, the development of a carefully studied biblical theology, and revelations of stark stupidity seem to make little difference in whether or not past dictums that need to be discarded continue to receive rapt attention.

Reactions to guilt have varied dramatically in my ministry. After watching persons recklessly pursue a course of self-destruction devoid of any caution signs or warning signals, I became convinced of the need to emphasize the positive aspects of guilt. Hearing disturbed individuals describe their complicity in wrongdoing and complain of guilt, I said, "You should feel guilt"—intending my statement as a helpful form of instruction, not as a rigid condemnation. During this period I came to understand the line in the Roman Catholic liturgy for the Saturday prior to Easter, "O happy guilt."

Soon, though, I began to see an avalanche of people whose morality was fragmented and faith tormented by superficial guilt, needless guilt (such people had been around me all along; only now was I able to see them). Their situation ("our" situation) was every bit as serious, in terms of spiritual health, as the plight of persons with no sense of guilt at all. Often respectable actions sprang from much less than noble, to say nothing of moral, motivations. Within myself I resolved never again to inflict guilt on people as a means of manipulation regardless of the lofty rightness of the goal.

How faithful I have been to the implementation of that resolution in relation to others, I am not sure. In the application of it to myself, I have failed miserably. Theological convictions and moral opinions always seem stronger as debatable propositions than as personal or social practices.

Experts on emotions identify guilt as a frequent contributor to some forms of depression. If so, depression should have come as no surprise to me. I shouldered a boxcar-load of guilt while, to make the situation worse, denying that guilt was a problem. Annoyed at myself intellectually (my knowledge was far superior to my actions), emotionally I succumbed to guilt created by situations over which I had no control and aggravated by thoughtlessly critical comments from frustrated individuals: "Visitors don't feel welcome in this church." "We are well under our budgeted goal for contributions for the year." "You know the Smiths joined another church in town." I listened attentively, tried to look pleasant, felt guilty, and became more depressed.

In most people's lives more than enough guilt emerges to keep them busy with healthy responses. Absolutely no reason exists to carry guilt dumped by hostile people or provoked by situations beyond personal control.

If guilt was a factor in the development of my depression, guilt was also encouraged by adverse effects from my depression. The two—guilt and depression—seem to reinforce each other. Finally, the mind is muddled, conscience is rattled, and actions become unpredictable.

An irrational pattern developed. Often I experienced guilt in relation to matters over which I had no control while sensing no guilt at all over situations that I could do something about. A dismal committee meeting that I chaired could provoke guilt while I never had a second thought about the lack of time spent with my family over several consecutive days. Guilt was prompted when a church member felt ignored. But God's command to rest was disregarded without the slightest twinge of conscience.

As depression deepened, the weight of the guilt increased, or vice versa. Sure, some of the guilt was appropriate, authentic. But not all of it. The doctor's diagnosis of hypertension spawned guilt. Any admission of depression made it worse. Education made little difference in this situation. I knew guilt was no more in order because of depression than because of a toothache. But chaotic emotions, not reason, were in charge.

Prolonged guilt, superficial or deep, can decimate a sense

of self-worth, erode much-needed confidence, destroy any awareness of security, and engender doubt about relief in the future. Grace and forgiveness are dominant doctrines in my theology. Repeatedly I have spoken of their reality and pointed to their possibility in relation to anyone. But in the darkness of this time period riddled by guilt, desperately needing to claim for myself the promises I had shared with others, they did not happen. Prolonged guilt had produced the predictable.

Perhaps in the very worst moments, someone could have helped, bestowed the assurance of pardon. However, I refrained from speaking of the guilt I felt and did not voice a request for help. I kept silent. That too made me feel guilty.

ANGER
"THAT REALLY MAKES ME MAD!"

"A good boy does not get angry or hang around people who do." So I was taught. Anger was labeled an ill-mannered, unwanted, morally offensive emotion. Getting mad at all was bad. Getting mad at an authority figure, especially a loved one, was almost inexcusable. Perhaps in someone's opinion I was supposed to be "above" anger. In reality, that was not the case. Since I was human, anger was a companion.

Predictably, in this environment, expressions of anger immediately had to acknowledge guilt as an escort. Self-inflicted guilt over feeling angry was enough of a problem to sustain rigorous attempts to avoid it. Imposed guilt could be expected when anger was expressed. Thus, much of the time anger was repressed and denied. That is one "childish thing" I continue trying to "put away."

Repressed anger retained without relief is dangerous— the proverbial rapidly ticking time bomb. Such anger does its destructive work one way or another.

A Vesuvius type of eruption is a possibility. Like lava

shooting up from the bowels of the earth, anger spews out of the depths of one's being with irrepressible force and uncontrollable fallout. Effects of this suddenly displayed anger can touch unsuspecting persons who have no idea of what is happening and set in motion reactions that increase the devastation.

An alternative is a slow seepage of anger, hardly noticeable to the undiscerning, almost never in amounts sufficient to cause alarm. When an inner rage surfaces in an almost negligible way, the fact that the wrath has an object may make no sense at all.

Anger may find only nonverbal, unrecognizable forms of expression—more respectable socially but more harmful physically. The results include serious headaches and stomach ulcers.

Finally, anger may exact the price for its presence from a person's emotions. Often, that means depression.

For most of my life, I have handled anger poorly. Typically, I display anger only among those whom I love. Thus, sadly, at times I have dumped emotional garbage on the very people who should always be the recipients of my best attitudes, words, and actions. Fortunately, no longer do my wife and our sons allow such misplaced anger to go unchallenged. I have been helped immensely by their refusal to receive from me anger that belongs somewhere else. All three of them will give a full day to serving as a sounding board for my talk about hurt and anger. But not one of them will devote one second to acting as a receptacle for emotional refuse I have collected among others.

Though taught to disdain angry explosions in public, sometimes I envy people who make no attempt to hide their wrath. Of course, some persons spew anger so easily and frequently that their behavior is obnoxious. I have no desire to emulate that disposition. Yet, I do find attractive the individual who can express justifiable anger toward others in a manner that is appropriate, honest, and respectful.

Wishing for such an ability dominates my thoughts when I

walk away from individuals and experiences that have provoked within me a legitimate anger which I have covered with a placid demeanor. Later, the unvented anger prompts a measure of disgust aimed at myself as I think: Why did I let those people get away with running all over me with their misinformation? Why did I not permit myself to show them how mad I felt? I am working on it.

For years, most of my anger has been repressed and seldom, if ever, discussed with anyone. Telling of my power at repression is a comment often heard from close associates: You never seem to get mad at anyone or anything. Little do they know. One person, though, is seldom, if ever, fooled— Judy, my wife. Refusing to allow me to get away with a charade, she perceptively interrupts a calm conversation with the observation, "You are really mad," and the question, "What or who is the cause of your anger?" Perturbed that my masquerading techniques have not been more effective, I feebly mumble, "Nothing" or, "Nobody." Sometimes my reply is indicative of the fact that I have fooled myself, if not her. "Oh, I didn't realize I'm angry."

Slicing through a thick, easily recognizable layer of depression to expose deeply buried, thus unrecognized, reservoirs of anger has required expert assistance. Sore spots of wrath have been isolated and examined with surgical exactness. Not always, though. Sometimes probing beneath the surface has resulted in the discovery of the presence of anger as a malignant mass defying any dissection, observation, or identification of its constituent parts.

Sources of my anger spanned a continuum stretched between the reasonable and the irrational. Physical, moral, and spiritual phenomena that frequently prompted wrath included disappointment, rejection, failure, fatigue, incompetence, hypocrisy, stupidity, disease, apathy, inflexibility, cowardice, legalism, and insensitivity. The specifics of the provocative situations involved avoidable accidents, bad judgments, harsh words, selfish actions, deliberately inflicted hurt, terminal illnesses, unavoidable problems, gaudy displays of self-righteousness, and evil efforts intended to accomplish good.

Personal objects of my anger included almost everyone. At the top of this list were persons looking out only for themselves, who, under the guise of genuine selfless care, used me as they had used others in pursuit of their goals and then, when finished, moved on to others for whom they could "care," others whom they could use. Among the recipients of senseless wrath were family members whose good counsel was mistaken for bad criticism, secretaries whose faithful efforts to keep me meeting appointments (which I had made) seemed like attempts to increase my fatigue, and church members whose normal requests sounded like unreasonable harassment. Logical anger was my reaction to persons whose support was limited to good times, to individuals whose friendship was too weak for fellowship in tough moments, to people whose positive words to my face were accompanied by mean criticisms behind my back, to folks who built themselves up by tearing others down, to groups that implied that perfection was a prerequisite to their acceptance. Conversely, I felt unreasonable anger toward people victimized by unfortunate circumstances, individuals whose lack of strength and courage was explainable by their past, churches that did not act like churches because of a failure to learn the nature of Christ's church, people whose destructive immaturity had developed apart from any challenge to grow.

Incidentally, few, if any, of these people ever knew of my anger toward them. Even so, I knew it well. Pushed down internally so I could be "nice" and pleasant externally, the anger developed into a rage.

Not the least among targets of my wrath and one of the most frequent was myself. Here again, logic and a lack of logic were often indistinguishable. I was mad at myself for being tired, for not liking what was likable, for not being able to express my deepest thoughts and feelings to those who cared most, for playing some of the ecclesiastical games invented by "professional church persons," for caring so much what other people thought about me, for refusing to rest, for not taking more time to study, for making bad decisions, for failing to take regular physical exercise, for getting sick, for being so angry, for gaining weight, for needing a doctor, for sinking deeper and deeper into depression. I really was mad.

Stringent efforts to hide this tumultuous anger, joined with constant attempts to appear as if all was well when nothing seemed well, made the situation worse. Self-interrogation was incessant: Why do I have to be so deceiving about feelings? What has happened to a life of peace? Why can I not, or why do I not, speak and act according to what I think and feel? Is the fault to be found in the inability of others to understand? Or is the difficulty explainable solely by the unrest, confusion, evil, lack of reason—some of that, none of that, or all of that—within me?

Exempt from my anger was God. (I am sure a heavenly sigh of relief must have escaped from the Divine Being, greatly relieved to know that!) Not intended as commendable—for in the final analysis the absence of anger toward God may not have been all that healthy—my confession is best understood as cowardice rather than piety. I am no match for God. That realization never has been in question.

Occasionally anger developed because of the consequences of living in the human situation with a certain controversial conviction attributed to divine revelation. At moments, I was ready angrily to denounce a theology that suddenly seemed incompatible with reality. Many times I walked away from a hospital room furious at the indiscretion of cancer cells or drove away from a cemetery with great indignation provoked by the prevalence of senseless tragedies and the deaths of innocent, good people. But my problem was not with God. I was mad at parts of God's world, some of God's church, and a few of God's creations in the divine image. My anger was not, however, directed toward God. I continued (and continue) to believe in a God of grace who desires good for all people.

In time, my anger got sick. And then, sicker still. Depression developed. Finally the anger and the depression became inseparably united.

GRIEF
"I HURT SO BAD!"

For thirty-eight years of my life grief was a prevalent condition observed among friends, a subject of study, and a need among parishioners which elicited sympathy and prompted ministry, but not a depths-plummeting personal experience. The death of an elementary-school classmate provoked security-threatening questions and fright rather than grief. During my early childhood, the deaths of two grandparents presented opportunities to see grief in each of my parents. However, I did not share this grief. For me, sadness was mingled with inquisitiveness, a relief that suffering had ended, pleasure at seeing out-of-town family members who gathered for funerals, and some guilt because I realized I was not feeling the kind of sorrow my parents exhibited.

My best friend from college and seminary days died of leukemia shortly after we completed graduate studies in different schools. The harshness of the impact of that loss was softened by innumerable conversations between the two of us in preparation for his final moment and a preference for death over the continuation of his radical deterioration. Grief was immediate. Sadness was profound. Indeed, I still miss Mack Taylor. However, the grief was not prolonged.

Grief can result from losses other than those caused by death. Intellectually, I knew that. But, experientially, I still had not been forced to deal with that reality.

How I personally would respond to a grief situation became a matter of real concern to me. As a parish pastor I regularly was in touch with people almost overwhelmed by grief—the death of a child, an injury that terminated a cherished career, bankruptcy, a surprise divorce, a son's rejection of and separation from his parents, the closing of an institution, the loss of a job. Often, as I ministered to grieving people, I wondered what my condition would be if roles were reversed. I knew the right words to speak and the proper actions to take, and both grew out of my faith. Grief-related ministries were never perfunctory. Yet I had not stood where these people stood. What if it were my job, my child, my parent lost? How, then, would faith fare? And what of hope?

An unexpected cardiac arrest caused the death of my father and removed my grief-oriented concerns from the realm of speculation. In an early-morning hour when the private phone in my office rang, I was thinking about acting surprised for a birthday party which I had discovered the church staff had planned for me that evening. Joy left quickly and stayed gone for a long time. After the doctor told me that my father was dead, I spoke briefly with my mother, who was devastated. Though I hurt badly, I assumed that I must play the part of the strong son. After all, I was a minister, a man of God.

Comfort from Judy and our sons was immeasurably significant, as were the caring responses from several close friends. For the most part, however, relationships and conversations with other people seemed to take rather than give, to weaken rather than strengthen. Not until the return to my mother's home after the funeral and burial did any of my grief surface. Even that was brief. Quickly I composed my emotions and did not allow them to emerge again during that stay with my mother.

When I returned to my home after several days of assisting my mother in the draining work that has to be done after the death of a spouse, my dominant thoughts centered on the well-being of my mother, now alone, and the mental-emotional status of our boys, with whom I had not had time alone. Considerations related to myself embraced only the professional agenda of an interrupted writing assignment to be completed, a sermon to be prepared for the following Sunday, and contacts that needed to be made. Right away my normal, fast-paced schedule resumed. Grief—the need for grieving and time for grieving—was ignored or repressed. Whichever it was, grief was delayed. I was not so much aware of being sad as of being tired, really tired.

Occasionally, the put-off grief that remained just beneath my surface emotions erupted. Frequently that happened while I was conducting a funeral. However, grief-bearing flashbacks and feelings screaming for attention were swiftly dismissed. "This is no time to think of myself; I must help this family." Sometimes the grief showed up unexpectedly. As a burning sensation spread through my body, I became acutely aware of the death of my father. Usually, though, my attention soon had to be directed elsewhere (at least, that is what I told myself).

A very helpful moment came during an uncomfortable telephone conversation with my mother. For months our talks had been dominated by her continued grief. My mother was not handling her grief with any more health than I was handling mine, though our methods were radically different. Many of her questions and comments disturbed me: "Can't you say something that will comfort me? You help other people all the time. Folks come to see you for counsel. Why can't you help me?" A long-overdue response finally was voiced. I said, "Mother, I can't help you. I know you lost your husband and that the loss hurts. I am sorry. But I lost a father. And I hurt too. I need to be able to grieve. You simply must reach out to your pastor or to someone else for assistance I can't give."

Within a family, being a family member is always more important than being a pastor to a family member. In the first place, one family member cannot pastor another family member very well. Second, one's identity as a pastor is not nearly so crucial as one's identity as a spouse, son, daughter, brother, or sister. Thus, in a family crisis, a pastor needs to be pastored, not pastoring.

The conversation with my mother was a turning point, a rare moment of health amid a worsening sickness. My mother asked for help and got her grieving over my father's death in proper perspective. I did not.

Almost two years passed before substantive grieving occurred. Too long? Of course. My wife knew I was in trouble before I did. When finally sadness spilled out and tears flowed, a dam seemed to break. The relief, much greater than any I had experienced previously, was temporary, however. By this time depression had begun. The specifics of death-related grief merged with the generalities of an undefined grief. At last joy returned. But often an occasion of happiness was followed immediately by a breathtaking downward plunge of emotions. Tears formed more easily than at any previous time in my life.

As with guilt and stress, so grief, which contributes to the strength of depression, also takes strength from depression. Distinctions between cause and effect are blurred, if not obscured.

My grief, fed by a variety of sources, continued. A realization of the absence of joyful fulfillment in ministry prompted grief over what had once been. Important relationships had been rocked by disappointments, rejection, and even betrayal. Destroyed dreams about the future of ecclesiastical institutions produced grief. Discoveries of reasons why once trusted friends could no longer be trusted prompted grief.

What seemed to be a reprieve from grief made possible by a geographical move did not last long. Memory played tricks on me, mean tricks. Only the positives of the preceding pastorate were recalled. Forgetting the ever-present worry, fatigue, discouragement, and restlessness that marked many of the last days in that situation, I began to grieve over the change. Any happiness associated with what I was doing was overshadowed by grief over the loss of what I had done. For the first time in my life, the past seemed brighter than the future. True or false, that thought, even if passing, is terrifying, grief-deepening, depressing.

My struggles with grief amid depression were worsened by one other major factor. Constant, cyclonic winds were storming through my denominational organization, destroying much of what had claimed my lifelong devotion. When that which had been torn down began to be rebuilt, I could not even recognize the replacements as compatible with my tradition.

In the late seventies, two men, one a minister and one a judge, announced a ten-year plan by which fundamentalists would take over the Southern Baptist Convention. Very few people took the threat seriously. I was one who did. For the next several years, along with colleagues who shared a concern regarding the fundamentalist threat, I devoted an inordinate amount of time and energy to attempts to check the success of the takeover movement. Grief and depression dogged the work of many of us.

Criticisms, rebukes, and remarks intended for character assassination from opponents were predictable and endurable. What hurt most were condemnation and rejection from friends within the convention—pastoral peers who complained that we were overreacting and institutional leaders whose very jobs and programs we were working to protect. For most of the decade of the eighties, my colaborers and I were told that we, not the takeover group, represented the real problem in our convention.

Seeking to sustain a national movement while continuing normal pastoral duties and familial responsibilities was too much for many of us. Important tasks and significant people were neglected. Perhaps a bit of compensation for that sad realization would have been experienced had our efforts resulted in any success. There was none. Repeated dashings of raised expectations of positive changes led to increased depression.

Depression can distort reason as well as emotions. Logic could not justify the amount of grief I carried over the decline (that is my judgment) of my denomination. Vacating the Texas pastorate necessitated my resigning from the executive committee of our convention. My position on this important body was filled by the judge who had designed the dismantling of the denomination intended to precede its transformation. He was now in a position to orchestrate even more effectively the demolition of what was and the construction of what he thought should be. Friends goodnaturedly joked with me about letting the fox into the chicken coop. They had no idea how their laughter cut like a knife, inflicting wounds aggravated by grief, a factor as dangerous as infection.

Well, the so-called "takeover" movement within my denomination took over. Ministry and missions priorities are being rewritten. Long-term position papers are being scrapped and new postures drafted, many of which are diametrically opposed to the previous positions. Friends are losing their jobs. Offerings are being redirected. Beloved professors, like the institutions in which they teach, are being harassed by heretic hunters. Worst of all, historic principles are being set aside by an allegiance to contemporary prejudices. Theology is brandished about as a sickle clearing a path along which religion can do commerce with a political agenda.

Grief over the loss of a denomination may seem strange, particularly when mentioned alongside grief provoked by the death of a family member. But I had been converted, baptized, and nurtured within this denomination. My mind had been challenged by the products of its presses. Later, my formal education was obtained from this denomination's excellent institutions and partially funded by its finances. Rich fellowship was inherent in denominational meetings. Professional goals included serving as a trustee or as a commissioner on certain denominational boards and agencies. For more than forty years this denomination had received my respect, tithes, energy, talents, and devotion. Then, in less than a decade, that denomination was gone. Informed insiders, fundamentalists and conservatives alike, agree that not in my lifetime will this convention ever again be as I have known it, loved it, and served it in the past.

Without intentional efforts at correction, grief combined with depression can deliver a real knockout punch. Depression tends to cause persons to turn their attention almost exclusively to themselves. Enter grief and a vicious cycle begins. Grief provokes self-pity, and self-pity deepens grief. "Woe is me. All of importance is gone. No one else ever has known such loss." Grief!

Out of bad experiences some good can come. Important truths emerged from my prolonged episode with intense grief—insights which if embraced in a timely manner could have prevented, and can prevent, needless dimensions of depression.

Words from a friend represent wisdom regarding my radically altered denomination. Maybe some of us loved it too much. In relation to authentic ministry, perhaps the means had become the end and passionate loyalty was misplaced.

Every significant loss demands an equally significant grief. At the time, nothing is more important than giving attention to reality and doing the grief work that is a necessity whatever the source (or sources) of the grief. To deny, repress, or delay dealing with grief is to risk sickness.

Often outside help is needed to achieve a satisfactory resolution of grief. Sometimes even helpers must have help.

DOUBT

"What's the use?"

In the church of my childhood, doubt was condemned as a tool of the devil. Questioning an affirmation of faith was the same as doubting it. So, in all church-related teachings, questions were to be resisted and doubts avoided. For a while I was obedient to that requirement. Early in life, however, I viewed such instruction as suspect.

Asking "Why" or "How do you know" was as natural for me as breathing. My curiosity recognized no sacred exemptions. Like many children, I raised questions related to basic biblical theology long before I knew either the significance of what I was asking or the spelling (much less the meaning) of "theology."

Education in critical methods of Bible study and historical debates in theology was a gift from God. Far from the faith-destroying results predicted by doctrinaire, anti-educational alarmists, such lessons led me into an enriched, deepened faith. Genuine joy accompanied the sense that at last I had found the freedom for the honest questioning and open thinking appropriate to faith centered in One who identified himself as "truth." Though neither questions nor doubts are desirable stopping places on the spiritual journey, both can be good friends encouraging greater faith along the way.

Never have I been fearful about my faith. Doubt has been unsuccessful in altering my basic beliefs about the sovereignty of God, the centrality of Christ, and the possibilities of redemption. Discussing faith assertions with skeptics, responding to questions intended to cause doctrinal difficulties, pursuing proper applications of biblical truths to complex contemporary situations, and seeking to develop a Christian apologetic that captures the interest of non-Christian thinkers always has been fun for me. Hard work, yes, but fun.

Faced with depression, everything was different. Questions that I encountered during my slide into depression and doubts with which I battled while depressed yielded nothing even close to fun, satisfaction, or fulfillment. Just the opposite.

The core of my religious faith remained solid. Even during the worst moments I had no desire to shake my fist at the heavens and shout denunciations at God or to jeer at the redemptive ministry of Jesus and flaunt a rejection of his teachings. Maybe I was just "chicken," without the stomach to risk additional trouble. But I think not. At the bull's-eye of the target of my doubt was me. Circling that center were people immediately around me. My sharp-pointed, dipped-in-poison arrows of doubt pierced the aimed-at areas with unusual accuracy.

Previously, self-doubt never had been a problem for me. Honest assessments of strengths and weaknesses created an awareness of what I can do well and what I had best leave alone. When working in areas of strength, I generally felt both confidence and strength. That changed.

As depression increased, self-esteem decreased and self-confidence all but disappeared. Suddenly I was questioning my ability to do tasks that previously had been done routinely. Second-guessing became a way of life. Did I say the right thing to that troubled counselee? . . . Maybe I should not have accepted this assignment; I'm not sure I can offer what they need. . . . Did my sermon fail to offer listeners immediate help? All of this was new, and profoundly disturbing.

Developments in one particular week stand out in my mind. Out of my own unending struggle with decisions about what is important, what is most valuable, and what biblical faith demands, I sought to share some conclusions with members of our congregation. Though depression was very heavy at the time, I experienced a measure of exhilaration as I wrote the sermon. I was writing autobiography as well as theology. Then, on Saturday, the day before the sermon was to be delivered, I began to question everything I had written. Sensing that the very convictions I intended to share with others were sources of pain and trouble for me, I balked, doubting that I should speak about these matters in worship. I told my wife I did not think I could do the sermon because I was no longer sure I believed its contents to be true. Oh, I thought the words were true, but the implications of those words could cause awful hurt. I wondered if I would not do best by my parishioners just to leave the status quo unquestioned and to allow truths shaped in secular molds to go unchallenged. After all, I thought, I don't want to cause anybody hurt. And I may be dead wrong. Well, I did the sermon on that Sunday morning, but neither the empty, perfunctory praise ("I enjoyed the sermon, Pastor") nor the more genuinely offered glowing affirmations ("One of the best statements of the gospel I have ever heard") from the listeners could calm the storm within my soul—a tearing, tornadic broadside formed from the clash of warm currents of joyful certainty and cold blasts of insecurity.

Unexpected, completely unpredictable actions among colleagues and friends destroyed a basic trust in other people that always had been of fundamental importance to me. Subsequently, some people charged me with an incredible naïveté. Others, probably more accurate and honest, put my attitude squarely within the category of stupidity. Nevertheless, the failure of other people to be who they had claimed to be was devastating. After kicking and screaming for a while in resistance, I finally succumbed to severe doubts (doubts which I did not and do not like), telling myself: You can't trust anybody. Everybody has a hidden agenda related to security and self-defense. An acknowledged bond of friendship can be abandoned without explanation when crisis comes to a relationship. Even among persons with shared commitments, the strength of discipleship appears to be dependent on the size of the problems to be confronted and the degree of popular acceptance expected.

Though my struggle had all the symptoms of a crisis of

belief, my major difficulties were known by their first and last proper names, not by theological labels. What I perceived to be broken promises, betrayals, disappointments, selfishness, anger, and hardheartedness relationally—in relation to unusually significant persons—shaped a powerful sense of failure and defeat theologically. My personal position was revealed in the rhetorical question, What's the use? If asked to explain, the words flowed like water rushing through a deteriorated, once-strong dam: "All I have thought to be important in life doesn't work, or if it does work for a while, it doesn't last long. Maybe none of it is true. Even individuals who say all the right words and affirm basic beliefs with which I concur cannot be counted on in a crunch. Crises drive us to a primitivism in which passionately watching out for one's own best interests prevails over all else." Of course, there were exceptional persons who stood over against my generalizations like giant exclamation marks. But I could not see them.

A combination of doubts about others and doubts about myself did serious damage to my certainty about the validity of gospel-shaped values. I did not stop believing in the primacy of grace and love, commending the advisability of openness and vulnerability, and advocating the elevation of individuals over institutions and mercy over law. I did, however, begin to question the survival possibilities of these values and of people committed to them within the church as well as the world. Allegiance to these priorities seems to invite an amassing of adversaries.

Eventually I began to associate my primal values with terrible pain. Doubts decimated convictions: Inevitably vulnerability will lead to abuse. Relate to others with grace and they will bombard you with judgment. Elevate the church in importance and you will hurt as you witness its devotion to decisions, programs, and goals far more secular than sacred. Open up to someone with real compassion and you will become the object of rejection. Being a friend to a person offers no assurance of being treated as a friend by that person. An internal conclusion—it doesn't work—took form externally in the critical question, "What's the use?" Then came my first-ever hesitation about ministry.

Forced to continue functioning while besieged with doubt-engendering questions, ministry becomes a burden. Responsibilities previously embraced are resented. Institutional and relational involvements once welcomed are avoided. Self-doubt bore into my soul like an unwieldy drill: I am a failure as a minister. Maybe all along I have hurt people more than helped them. Perhaps I should leave the ministry. I don't want to do that, but how can I function like this? If people knew the depth of my struggles, they would not want me as their minister anyway.

Prominent in my thoughts at this point was the allurement of that damnable social principle which determines worth by professional position: I have been held in high esteem because I have been appointed to important jobs. Where will I be if that is gone? I don't know what people really think about me. Perhaps folks have appreciated where I have been much more than who I am. I fought these thoughts vigorously, but untruth won: In all honesty, maybe I am worth very little.

Depression deepened.

WHAT YOU KNOW CAN HURT YOU

"If you knew all that, why didn't you do something about it?" Knowledge is not the issue. A student of depression can become a victim of depression. What you know can hurt you without a conscious awareness that you are being hurt. Even as my condition worsened, I was convinced I was all right. Understanding depression and avoiding depression are two very different matters.

Analytical descriptions can be deceptive. What you have been reading is the product of careful reflection and studied attempts at a helpful organization of thoughts for purposes of clarification. In my experience, however, at no time were the factors that contributed to my depression ever so isolated, so clearly identifiable in nature, and so easily discernible from each other as may be suggested by this text.

Commonly, moods were complex and emotions confused. Grief and anger became so intermingled that frequently one was indistinguishable from the other. The wear and tear of prolonged guilt felt like symptoms of extensive physical fatigue. Destructive stress was buried so deeply in my emotions that the demands of daily schedules seemed to be the only explanation for relentless painful pressure. Anxiety mounted and encouraged doubt. Doubt could set off guilt, grief, or anger. Amid such an emotional mess, efforts at correctives were often directed toward the wrong problem.

My passion for reason was rebuffed repeatedly. Finally, while I was in the hospital, an experienced doctor urged me to quit trying to make sense of everything. No one ever had said that to me before. I had been trained to try to make sense of everything. To my surprise, the doctor observed that my difficulties were being compounded by my inability to deal with the irrational. He emphasized that my powers of logic would remain impotent as resources for help. I tried to make sense of that. Unsuccessfully.

Then there was the matter of chemical imbalance cited by three different doctors as the major culprit behind my depression. I understood the principle behind this explanation as presented in medical texts on depression, but coping with that as a personal problem was an entirely different situation. Besides, in my case, the medication I was taking at the time for correction seemed to worsen the illness.

For one of the first times in my life, what I knew did not matter. Though able to see and to relate to depression in others, I had been blind to and unable to cope with depression in myself. Logic, a tool on which my education had made me dependent, was virtually irrelevant.

"THERE IS NO PEACE AND JOY!"

By-products of depression can be as hurtful as the depression itself. Paranoia became a problem for me.

One afternoon while I was still a pastor, an older lady in our congregation stopped by my office to say she was praying for me. She explained that in recent days she had not been able to get me out of her thoughts. Sensitivity to the possibility of problems in my life had led to this visit. Inside, I panicked. Does she know how depressed I am? Has she picked up on the magnitude of my struggles? Is my discomfort readily apparent throughout the church?

After my hospitalization and subsequent resignation from the pastorate, paranoia intensified. Not receiving phone calls from certain people raised questions about their continued friendship. At the same time, rings of the telephone incited an irrational fear of bad news. Not only did I not want to answer the telephone, I did not want to receive caring visitors. Why have they come? Are they here to say something bad or hurtful? During one stretch of time, I did not go to the mailbox because of a worry that I might receive negative correspondence. Just enough fulfillments of my paranoid expectations occurred to make the situation worse.

Old stories about paranoid people were no longer heard as laugh-inducing jokes. When I saw people talking, I feared they were talking about me. I preferred to stay away from large crowds. Even a room filled with friends was intimidating.

A variety of rumors were making the rounds. At one extreme was the charge that I really was in good health and that my reported illness had been faked as a cover-up for problems at the church; at the other extreme were mixed-up reports about a severe illness, defined by some as a "life-shattering" breakdown and reported by others as bypass heart surgery. Not all the rumors dealt with health. I heard that my wife and I were divorced. Charges not based on facts know no boundaries. So every encounter with people prompted discomforting musings: I wonder what they have heard. Will I have to undergo a series of probing questions? Are these people going to turn their backs on us?

Paranoia makes peace impossible. Life is miserable. I despised the phenomenon. Intellectually, I could see through it. But emotionally I could not get away from it. Then, too, periodic episodes in which a relatively enjoyable tranquillity was interrupted by a painful brush with blatant untruths served to make sickness look like health, to encourage a confusion between destructive, abnormal paranoia and normal perceptions of reality. "Everybody is talking about me," I felt I could say honestly. "Some people really are attempting to do me in."

Equally difficult, though neither constant nor predictable, were anxiety attacks. No warnings preceded them. No circumstances were sure to cause them. No specifics explained them. Most moments of intense anxiety lacked any recognized reasons for the condition.

When radical anxiety showed up, a ticker tape of issues wound its way through my mind and emotions: worry over relationships—what is wise and what is unwise, how to be fair, questions about the nature of authentic love; a variety of security concerns—financial needs, future professional possibilities, disappointments related to friends; self-interrogation—Are my good gifts shot? Have I closed the door on any possibility of fulfillment in the future?; family-oriented self-accusations—How badly have I harmed my wife? Have I made life difficult for our sons? Why must my family members suffer negative consequences of my sickness?

Sure, I knew well Jesus' words about avoiding anxiety. But when the anxiety attacks came (uninvited and unwelcomed), obedience to that admonition from the Lord seemed at best in the service of sheer survival and at worst impossible. Usually, these episodes of extreme anxiety did not last long, though their effects lingered. Not infrequently, a bout with anxiety was joined by a dangerous mixture of guilt and anger.

In many respects, the worst of all the depression-related difficulties was the loss of joy. For a period of four or five years, I could not remember what it was like to be happy. Several times I asked family members if they could recall previous periods of our life together in which I seemed happy. Combined with a lack of memory of sustained joy in the past was an inability to hope for a recovery of joy in the future. Often I wondered, Will I, or maybe more accurately, *can* I ever be happy again?

My immediate family prizes celebrations. Throughout our lives together, first the two of us, then three, and then the four of us have seized significant moments and surrounded them with festivities. A capability for festivity remained in my head but not in my heart. For the sake of others, I could speak and act in a manner commensurate with a celebration while feeling little or no joy myself. I despised such an existence.

During this difficult stretch of time, occasions for fun and laughter did occur. My contribution to such experiences was almost exclusively reaction, not initiation. Unexplainably, even when humorous thoughts entered my mind, I was unable to voice them. Also, those rare moments when I sensed true happiness, when I knew something of joyous abandon, ended with the abruptness and pain associated with a fall after running full speed into a brick wall. The higher the summit of joy briefly scaled, the lower the valley of depression into which I immediately fell.

"I-talk" bothers me. The prevalence of the first-person pronoun in this book is necessitated by the autobiographical nature of its material. During my illness, however, an unyielding focus on "me" dominated countless days, symptomatic of as well as a contributor to my depression. Experts state that the deeper one sinks into depression, the more preoccupied the person becomes with the "self."

Reason and emotions waged another futile battle. Hypochondriacs repulse me. Over the years, I have emphasized to counselees that not everyone wants to see their scars—products of either physical surgery or emotional wounds. Yet I could not seem to get my thoughts off my hurts and hush my verbal complaints. Repeated recitals of my pains must have wearied members of my family. With my mind, I knew better, resolving to cease the regular medical briefings on myself. But knowing differed from doing. Correct information does not guarantee correct action. Apparently I did not want anyone to get the idea that they could feel worse than I did. So from the depression came a preoccupation with myself which I found as unending as it was disgusting—and further depressing.

Days varied in quality. A wearisome heaviness never left. Anxiety always seemed ready to eradicate any thoughts of security. After increases in the amounts of medication prescribed, a fog shrouded my personhood—emotions were dulled and clear thoughts prevented. Even so, at times duties were dispatched efficiently. Long hours of work were not a problem. Positive developments even occurred in the realm of my ministry.

Dominant, though, were days ruled by depression. I did not want to get out of bed in the morning because I did not think I could get through the day. Preparation for going to the office was accompanied by complaints: "I don't believe I can do it today. I'm too tired to get up and go." Negotiating early-morning traffic was a major task not done very well (Judy said she could tell the level of my depression by the way I drove). Lifting a foot to take a step required great effort. Many times I shuffled more than walked. A bent back, slumped shoulders, and a drooped head constituted a body language that accurately indicated inner feelings. Once settled into the security and comfort of my office, I wanted no interruptions other than those few I chose. Much time not spent restacking papers on my desk meaninglessly was spent sitting quietly and staring into space. Constant pain had taken up residence in my head.

Ordinarily I could psych myself up to meet appointments and make telephone calls. Concentration on visitors' comments required studied efforts. Administrative dilemmas requiring decisions became real bothers. What I did best was relate to people plagued by problems.

Numerous individuals praised my accurate perception of the dynamics of their feelings of guilt, anger, doubt, futility, sadness, rejection, and depression. "You have read my mind," they said, or, "How can you know me so well?" Little did they realize that listening to their concerns was like hearing myself talk while looking in a mirror.

Such a situation is fraught with the potential for relational dangers. When an individual who generally feels misunderstood and not properly cared for by people seen as insensitive (whether or not that is actually the case) finds another individual who demonstrates sensitive concern, expresses a willingness to help, and establishes immediate rapport, strong feelings of bonding can develop. It is not a one-way street. When the pastor/teacher/counselor (helper) is also struggling with turbulent emotions, he or she can reach out to the counselee in an unhealthy manner. From the "person on the couch" can come the acceptance, affirmation, and even adoration sought by the "person behind the desk," thus lifting a sagging self-esteem and eliciting positive feelings that have almost been forgotten. Unexpectedly, the emotional difficulties in one or both of the persons are seemingly transcended for a glorious moment. Without discipline, essential boundaries between professional concerns and personal interests can be crossed quickly and thoughtlessly. Reason can be tossed aside and feelings enthroned even within basically nonfeeling persons.

In my situation, the relational ravages of depression were greatest within my family. All along, my wife, Judy, could see clearly what I could hardly, if ever, see at all. Time and time again, she questioned my decisions, suggested significant changes in my work habits, warned of dangers in my judgments, and urged me to seek additional professional help. Almost invariably I heard her wise, well-intended words as harsh criticisms and condescending judgments. I reacted negatively—either in an outburst of anger or by way of psychological, if not physical, withdrawal. What she offered as helpful, I accepted as hurtful. Thus, instead of Judy's words and actions driving me toward professional assistance, which would have been logical, they drove a wedge between the two of us, an illogical development.

Judy did not understand. As she watched me work professionally and relate socially she saw a sensitivity to a wide variety of people, a willingness to share openly (at least that was the appearance), laughter, energy, and devotion. At home she saw little of any of that. Not aware of how much I was faking everything in relation to others, she assumed I just did not care anything about relationships at home. Naturally, that provoked hostility and hurt.

At times I must have seemed bent not only on the destruction of myself but on a totally adverse alteration of life for the people around me, the people who mattered most to me—though for the life of me I could not let them know that, even in those infrequent moments of sanity when I knew it. I shut out friends. I ignored indebtednesses. I jeopardized our security. And I resented any reminder of or question about the negative consequences of my inaction.

I made virtually no contributions to our family life during this period. I was away from home often. I had no interest whatsoever in domestic concerns. Normal responsibilities went unattended. Conversations were avoided. No declarations or demonstrations of affection were offered. Physically and emotionally, literally and metaphorically, I turned my back on the very people whose arms were open to me.

Predictably, rejection and disinterest, rebuffs of expressions of love, can be endured just so long. Tired of hurt, Judy finally, in self-defense, said she was ready to quit trying. I do not know how she persisted with such patience for so long. My behavior was humiliating her as well as hurting her. During one stretch of time Judy decided that what was wrong with me was not only an illness called depression but a lack of marital devotion, an irresponsible escapism, and a deplorable selfishness. On the basis of appearances alone, she could make a good case for her conclusion.

Repeatedly, Judy said she was going to quit trying to work on our relationship, to give up on me. Both would have been justifiable and understandable. But, I am thankful to say, she never did either one. Strengthened by an awareness that I was sick, and somewhat knowledgeable of depression, she refused to give up hope for a better day for the two of us and a complete recovery for me.

Reviewing the past with a reemergence of clarity in thoughts and feelings during my recuperation, I am astounded at my wife's strength of character (which, when acknowledged by some, will no doubt be categorized as unhealthy too). Judy has demonstrated more commitment, courage, grace, and hope than I ever could have imagined. That does not mean I see my wife as perfect. Sometimes her outbursts of justifiable anger aggravated the tension already between us. The needless guilt that she imposed on herself, trying to be responsible for situations for which she was not responsible, lowered her self-esteem and weakened the bond between us. Occasional misperceptions of depression resulted in her voicing words of encouragement that had a negative impact on my condition. However, I shudder to think of what a dramatic difference in circumstances could have developed had the situation generally, and our roles, specifically, been reversed.

For me, relief from depression came in writing and speaking. Though at the time I was not fully aware of what I was doing, during some of the worst periods of depression my writing and speaking were filled with discussions of the life I wanted to be living. The feelings I wanted to experience, I could only describe in writing and preaching.

In the midst of a great deal of misery, I completed a manuscript eventually published as *God's Clowns*. Working on this project often brought the only joy on mostly joyless days. My writing majored in what I feared had been minors in my life. Delight developed as I wrote about running and shouting, dancing and singing, vulnerably establishing intimacy, taking risks, and living out dreams, though at times I was afraid I lacked the strength required to push the pen across the page to form my thoughts into words.

A look at my preaching from this time period reveals the same tendency. Most every one of the factors just treated in this book as sources of depression appeared as healthy affirmation in my sermons. Weak to the core of my being, I talked about strength. Weary and unwilling to stop working, I commended the Sabbath principle of rest. Bombarded by guilt, I lauded the centrality of grace. Often racked with rage, I described the benefits of a proper release of anger. Defensively cautious, I praised vulnerability. Feeling boxed-in, I explored liberty. Profoundly sad, I elaborated the possibilities of C. S. Lewis's popular phrase "surprised by joy." Sermonic paragraphs abounding with "hallelujahs" were written in hellish seasons.

Such lack of cohesion is not easily sustained. On numerous occasions I walked to the pulpit after sitting in my office shaking and weeping. The sermons delivered in those situations communicated effectively and offered no indication of personal problems. Immediately, though, I realized that enough strength for a week was expended in getting through that one hour. But sleep and rest could not replace what was lost. More importantly, the integrity of personal wholeness was being eroded dramatically. For that, too, I was not sure any help was possible.

"WHAT NOW?"

Though I have experienced depression, I do not understand depression. My sympathies are with those physicians who characterize the disorder as a mystery. Completely unclear to me (but I am not alone) is the relationship between a person's emotional reactions to external situations and the biochemical developments that take place in a person's brain in the development of depression. For example, some individuals cope with stress admirably and still become depressed. In the chemical-emotional equation, can one factor without the other cause depression? Or are both required? Is depression more the product of a chemical imbalance, which must be treated pharmaceutically, or a psychosis, which must be addressed by psychotherapy?

Potential contributors to depression continue in my life. In fact, I do not want to be without them. Every phenomenon that when abused contributed to depression, and which when influenced by depression worsened, is valued. The absence of any one of them would diminish significantly the meaning of life.

Guilt is a helpful response to sins in need of recognition and eradication as well as forgiveness. Little that is important is accomplished without a measure of stress. Anger is a healthy emotion, highly commended by the Bible and properly provoked by all kinds of evil. Grief is the price of love. Protection from grief would be an obstruction to authentic compassion. Doubt can be among faith's best friends.

Not even by implication do these observations constitute a suggestion that I am now the master of all these emotions. Far from it. At times anger still threatens to race toward rage before I can recognize it and get it in check. Periodically, grief surfaces, causing grave sadness over severed relationships, lost opportunities, fractured friendships, misunderstandings, and mistakes. Self-doubt is dying a slow death. In no sense do I have it made. Potential for the abuse of an emotion, however, is no reason to deny the presence of that emotion or to avoid the proper use of it.

All right, Miss Dunn—for that matter, all right, everyone—honest confession *is* good for the soul.

3
Who's Crazy Here?

A sign on the locked door within the hospital warned of detention devices, equipment to prevent efforts at an unexcused escape from the area. I saw it immediately, but quickly shifted the focus of my eyes, hoping that the posted information had not registered in my brain or stirred my emotions. Pushing a small buzzer activated an intercom through which I identified myself to an unseen voice and requested entrance into the mental-health unit as a patient. My wife, friend, and I made our way straight to the nurses' station. I walked hesitantly and stiffly, looking neither to the right nor to the left.

A very pleasant, outgoing therapist greeted me and indicated that she would be conducting my orientation to the unit and an intake interview. Another nurse took my one piece of luggage and my briefcase. (Yes, my briefcase. I could not even go to the hospital without a briefcase. I took along books and notepads, with every intention of setting up an office in my room and dealing with business matters that needed attention.) She explained that the items would be returned to me after their contents were examined. Electrical appliances, an electric razor and a hair dryer, were exceptions; each would have to be checked out as needed and immediately returned for safekeeping. Quickly I got the idea that I was facing a set of circumstances unlike any I had encountered before. I did not know the half of it.

After hurried good-byes to my wife and to the friend who drove me to the hospital, I sat down with the therapist, who was armed with a long list of questions for me to answer. She began by saying, "Welton," and then explaining that everyone in this unit speaks to each other on a first-name basis. I bristled a bit. I'm accustomed to being addressed as "Dr. Gaddy" when I go to the hospital. What about a recognition of my position? I worked hard to get a "Dr." before my name, I found myself thinking. "That's fine," I replied to her.

Once the therapist launched into the prescribed interrogation, I resolved: All right, I am here. I must make the most of this. No cover-ups. Say what you think. Express what you feel. Intending all of that and doing it are two very different matters. But I tried. As we moved from the perfunctory information about family, education, job, and the like to subjective responses which required debatable interpretations, value judgments, and personal opinions, I found myself laboring hard. Already I was discovering how much my typical daily conversations are filled with calculated comments which are acceptable, vague statements intended to answer a person's question without enough specificity to cause a negative reaction, and carefully chosen words which reek with professional authority but completely hide personal sentiments.

I realize this initial interview was intended for the benefit of the hospital staff. However, it helped me. What was conveyed implicitly was far more important than any of the words explicitly spoken. I recall thinking, These people are serious. They are taking seriously both me and my situation. I can tell them exactly how bad things are for me without fear of a reprimand or rejection. No need exists to try to fool these folks by saying what seems most acceptable and forcing actions aimed at eliciting affirmation. They are specialists who have heard it all and seen it all before. Efforts at deception may delay an accurate diagnosis of my state of being, but eventually they will be recognized for what they are—indicators of my hesitation to describe a quiet desperation. Maybe I can find help; maybe I can be helped here. I was beginning to make an important transition into a virtually all-new kind of world.

A walk through the different areas of this hospital unit was intended to familiarize me with locations which, for various reasons, would be important to me in the days ahead—where to deposit and pick up items for the laundry, where to find snacks, where to watch television. (I had looked forward to large segments of time alone for reading and for watching television. I felt that I needed the time alone as much as I liked it. The therapist explained that patients' rooms do not have televisions in them because depressed people tend to want to spend too much time alone. "They think of everything!" I said to myself with disgust. "I'm sure they are right, but I don't like their rule." However, they did not ask my opinion, and they were in charge, not I.) I made mental notes regarding the most essential places in the unit—pharmaceutical dispensary, kitchen, dining room, group-therapy room, living room, nurses' station. But while moving around the area, I was far more conscious of the people I saw than of the instructions I heard.

Few of the patients spoke initially. That was all right with me. Actually, I preferred not speaking. I felt more like looking for a soundproof shell to hide in. But the physical-emotional demeanor of the people struck me and resounded within me like shouts. One lady sat sleeping before the blaring television, occasionally jerking and snoring. Two residents seemed caught up in a whispered conversation. An older woman moved constantly, whispering to herself all the while. From a room down the hall came a scream. Two teenage boys stood in sharp contrast to each other—one neatly groomed and dressed in a robe, gliding around the unit comfortably, speaking to people lightheartedly, and exuding confidence; the other far more disheveled in

appearance—torn jeans, floppy shirt, long unkempt hair—
sat slumping over, seemingly brooding angrily, hostilely,
resentfully, or with some other negative emotion. All these
people—some with obviously severe emotional disorders—
looked as if they needed to be here. But me?

As the therapist and I continued to move about, I overheard a conversation that dealt with "going home." A young
man had announced in a loud voice, "I'm supposed to go
home tomorrow, but I think I'm going to ask the doctor if I
can stay at least one more day. I don't believe I'm ready yet."
Someone else spoke up with a hope of going home by the
end of the week. Eventually I learned that talk about
"getting out" and "going home" never ceased. That particular night, however, my first night, the conversation hit me
like a gunshot. Like blood rushing to a wound, thoughts
rushed to my head: I don't believe I can take this talk about
going home when I am just getting here. I would never tell a
doctor I wanted to wait even one extra hour before being
released from this place.

I wanted to go home, but I also wanted to get well. I
dreaded the thought of an extended hospitalization, but
already I did like the friendly, nonthreatening environment
of the ward and the protection from additional adverse
pressures from the outside. Could I, would I, like the young
boy, get to a point of wanting to stay in the hospital longer?
"How long is this going to take?" That was the recurring
question from which I could not escape.

"Are we allowed to make phone calls?" I asked. For
someone accustomed to spending several hours each day
talking on the telephone, that is a crucial question. Relief,
with perhaps a little encouragement, arrived when I was told
that both local and long-distance calls could be made night
and day.

After nervously picking at the cool contents of a dinner
tray that had been held for me for two hours, I rushed to the
phone excited as if I never had known the privilege of
placing a phone call. I called home. "How was the trip back?

Did you stop to eat? Was the traffic heavy?" Those were the words that came out of my mouth. Inside, though, the contents for another conversation were ready to be sounded: Are you sure this is all right? What do you expect to happen? What's next? For the first time that whole day, emotions surged to near eruption, my voice broke, and tears flowed. After mumbling a needless, ridiculous statement, "Don't forget me," I said good-bye, hung up the phone, and went to my room.

Over the next several days the institutional surroundings became less and less significant and the individual hospital patients more and more important. The change did not take place outside of me or within those around me. Something different was going on in me.

I was not totally unfamiliar with the phenomenon. More than once after arriving in a city to keep an out-of-town speaking engagement when the schedule at home has been hectic, I have been driven to a motel, checked into a room, told that I had several hours of free time, and then—nearly panicked. Suddenly there was no need for the powerful internal motor which for days had been running constantly at a high speed. I did not know how to turn off that indomitable drive so necessary to realizing accomplishments, so detrimental to sustaining good health. I did not know what to do. I had trouble sitting down, lying down, or even walking leisurely. I had the strong sensation that something needed to be done. Only after hours of unwinding could I enjoy the absence of stress. Often much the same scenario has accompanied past vacations. Only after two or three days of transition could I allow myself to be still and to enjoy relaxation.

An early frustration in the hospital developed because of my penchant for checking calendars, keeping schedules, and moving through the day knowing what to expect from one hour to the next. Several times during the orientation session I interrupted the therapist with questions: "Is the schedule here the same every day? What are mealtimes? Will the doctors always visit at prescribed hours? Do the therapy groups have set meeting times and agendas?" More than ever before, I became conscious, uncomfortably conscious, of my need for structure (structures may be more accurate— structures of time, authority, relationships, and problem-solving). Only with difficulty did I adjust to plans for a day not being announced until after breakfast on that very day. And some days the workers forgot to write down the schedule for all to see.

Maybe the importance of the people around us never can be recognized adequately until other matters—schedules, agendas, arrangements—recede in importance. That was my experience. Once I had begun to relax, to move without the compulsion appropriate for fighting a fire, to respond to the makeup of each moment, I started to notice people.

I was surrounded by interesting individuals. A nice-looking fifteen-year-old boy had major problems with anger. One day he broke a door. Another teenager, this one not well groomed or attractive, also battled anger. At times he withdrew from everyone, seething with resentment and boiling with rage. A young, deeply troubled Hasidic Jewish woman fluctuated dramatically in her moods and appearance. At times neat and attractive and at other times the epitome of disarray, this little lady was intimidated by images of the perfect Jewish mother, cautiously frustrated by the requirement of submissiveness to her husband, and completely overwhelmed by the demands of her three children, aged three, one, and two-and-one-half weeks. A middle-aged woman who maintained a professional appearance seemed to enjoy the hospital. On several occasions she received passes to leave the grounds for dinner with her husband, but each time she displayed great pleasure on her return to confinement. A truck driver near the same age as this woman remained an enigma. An older woman kept in constant motion (literally), relentlessly whispering to herself, "Get me out of here. Get me out of here." Two rough-in-demeanor women had coughs that sounded symptomatic of the last stages of a deadly bronchitis, yet almost every time I saw them they were smoking cigarettes.

By no means were these all the people I encountered as colleagues under care. During my entire hospital stay, though, only two people were separated from the rest of us and confined alone—a man in mid-life, who kept beating on the locked door of his room, yelling, and taking off all his clothes, and a young man who imagined himself to be a major rock star and attempted an escape on the staff elevator. However, both these people were quickly reintegrated into our little community.

Paying careful attention to the people around me, I started to notice their peculiarities, to ponder their comments, to hear even their throwaway words, to watch their expressions, to appreciate their eccentricities, and to be comfortable with them either in the fellowship of silence or conversation. Though some characteristics of the residents of this community of illness were humorous and others sad, still others were beneficial, helpful, worthy of emulation, even—I hesitate to use the word—healthy.

Often I pondered the question, Who is crazy here and who is healthy? What began as playful inquisitiveness developed into a seriousness pregnant with beneficial insights. Growing out of repeated reflections on that topic, here is an itemization of some aspects of our (I first wrote "their") life together—the actions and attitudes of a few hospital patients—that could contribute substantially to the improvement of all our lives together as humans.

GIFTS OF ACCEPTANCE AND TOLERANCE

Though the people in my new place of abode did not rush toward me with prolific greetings (thank goodness), they did want me to know their names, first names, and to share my name. These exchanges were made quietly, as I encountered various persons while moving about the unit. Acceptance here seemed to come with the territory. I felt no pressure to be somebody in particular—an answer man, a problem solver, a spiritual resource, an administrator—in order to be acceptable and welcomed. I was accepted; no big deal.

As I surveyed the area with my eyes and in my mind wondered about the different people present, I felt real ambivalence about conversations. A part of me wanted everyone to ask, "Who are you, really?" a question that I would interpret as, "What do you do?" I was eager to distinguish myself from the others: "I am a respected minister. I am an important person. I am here not so much because of major weaknesses as overexpended strengths." (Would they have laughed? That would have been appropriate.) But also within me was a desire for people to make no inquiries whatsoever—to just let me be.

During that first evening in the hospital, no one other than the professional staff asked me about anything except my name. Days passed before anyone inquired about my work. Then the topic was an incidental aside in a casual conversation, not a major concern. Acceptance into the fellowship of these people was independent of position, abilities, accomplishments, or potential.

Amazingly absent as well was an interest in the reasons for a person's hospitalization. No one asked, "What was the breaking point for you? What was the final straw? Did you do something dangerous, immoral, or irrational?" Attitudes about admissions were inconsequential, whether one wanted to be here, chose to be here, or was forced to be here against personal will. Presence was the basis of acceptance.

I do not recall any prior preparation or precedent for this experience. My acceptance into and involvement with groups has tended to be related directly to positions and actions. Everybody knew why everybody else was there. If not, the opening moments of a meeting were devoted to all present identifying themselves and their work. Credentials and potential were crucial concerns. All present were aware

that acceptance into the group had been earned and continued participation in the group would have to be merited.

Tolerance was as much a given as acceptance in this
hospital unit. One woman slept most of the day every day.
Another paced the floor. A young woman worked constantly
with her hands. An older woman read a great deal. Some
watched television for long hours at a time. Two or three
newfound friends clustered for conversation. One person
wept incessantly. Not once did I see anyone raise an
eyebrow questioningly or critically about someone else's
behavior or hear anyone make a derogatory comment regarding it.

At times I like to sit in silence—reading, watching television, thinking, or just resting. However, I never have felt very
comfortable doing that in the presence of other people.
Pressures, imagined or real, demand a contribution to the
company present. If you are going to be with people
physically, you must at least act interested in them and
attempt to draw them into a conversation—so went my
thoughts. That attitude was altered among the hospital
patients. I found great comfort and peace in being able to sit
alongside people feeling no obligation to look a certain way
or to speak a certain word in order to please them. One older
gentleman and I frequently sat together on the couch for
long stretches of time never exchanging a word with each
other and never feeling worse about each other because of it.
The need for tolerance never had to be explained. Maybe it
was anticipated. Whatever the case, tolerance was granted.

What great good gifts—acceptance and tolerance! No
wonder these two traits are dominant among the
characteristics of the people of God as biblically understood.
Subtly in his parables and overtly in his actions, Jesus
demonstrated the radical openness inherent in the divine
invitation to fellowship—fellowship with God and with all
God's people. Neither moral perfection nor physiological
wholeness was made a prerequisite for acceptance. In fact,
depictions of God's people were often almost humorous.

What a collection of failures, cripples, and outcasts; poor-sighted, frequently scorned, and sin-bent people! Of such is the kingdom of God. (The period after the preceding sentence is a compromise between an insistent need for an exclamation point and thoughts about the appropriateness of a question mark.)

What a fellowship is formed when acceptance and tolerance are practiced. Local churches can learn a great deal about such a fellowship, both from the pages of the New Testament and from the patients in a mental-health facility such as the one of which I was a part.

Imagine the positive difference that could be made in people's lives if they were encouraged to be themselves, spared acceptance based on performance, and extended tolerance in the face of even radical uniqueness. Stress-related difficulties could be reduced significantly, the general level of people's self-esteem raised appreciatively, and relaxation experienced regularly. Why are such life-enhancing acceptance and tolerance more prevalent among people who do not speak of faith and compassion than among persons who boast of a compassion born of faith? Why are these good gifts more characteristic of people declared to be ill than among folks judged to be healthy?

BEAUTIFUL EQUALITY

It was impossible to determine how radical the equality was in that hospital community. No means were available to the patients for evaluating the degree of diversity represented there. Widespread diversity is a safe bet, however.

Readily apparent, of course, were racial differences. Careful attention during group conversations often picked up incidentally dropped indications about the lifestyle of an individual—whether or not she lived alone, what kind of recreation he enjoyed, how much education had been achieved, past experiences of travel. When patients' family members came to the ward during visiting hours, often they provided evidence regarding the religious preferences, business interests, and affluence or poverty of their hospitalized relative. Enough was known about the diversity inherent in the community to make its practice of equality a thing of beauty.

Equality was real. On most days a community meeting was held to hear announcements and to plan activities. Everybody in the unit was invited to these sessions. When decisions were made by a majority vote, everybody was encouraged to participate. No one was told, "You are too ill, too young, too old, too illogical, or too much of a problem to offer your opinion regarding this decision." The same standard prevailed in other situations as well.

Though, by doctors' orders, individual diets might vary as to their content of sodium or sugar, concentration of fat, or inclusion of meat, at mealtimes everyone ate together. No one had a designated table or was provided special dining-room privileges of any kind. Glances around the table during dinner revealed only minimal distinctions between the persons present.

Exceptions of any kind were scarce. All patients served on a committee, though each person was allowed to choose a specific assignment—the welcoming committee, the clean-up committee, or the roundup committee. All patients received their medication and consulted with their physicians in the same manner. All patients were expected to abide by the same rules regarding quiet times and times for retiring to bed in the evenings and getting up in the mornings. All residents were included as full participants in the daily therapy groups. Always speaking to one another on a first name basis, patients did not assign to one another a superior or inferior status. If participation in some planned activity required an expenditure of money that a patient did not have, funding for that purpose could be requested confidentially without the reason for need being questioned. Exclusion was avoided and equality protected.

Strange. Who would imagine that the "equality under law" lauded by our most basic civil documents and the "equality under grace" commended and commanded by Jesus Christ would be implemented most dramatically among people considered by many "not quite right"! Yet here in the mental-health unit of a hospital, among people sometimes labeled as aberrations of society, was the realization of one our society's most elusive aspirations.

And the church's commission. Among the people of God, what reason exists for anyone to pull rank, to eat at the "head table," to assume a unique importance? An indisputable form of equality within the church is a reality whether or not it is recognized and practiced. No person is a member of the church because of a superiority to other persons. All people in the church are there because of a fundamental need for God. In any community of God's people, two certainties persist—life can be put right for anybody and something is wrong with everybody.

Among my institutionalized peers in pursuit of good health, no one seemed to have to strain or struggle to respect equality as a principle or to evidence it in actions. And, by the way, no one—neither hospital patient nor medical professional—declared that it had to be this way. I did not hear the word "equality" mentioned even once. This is just the way things were. In this setting, equality was not so much a noble concept of ideology as a fundamental, behavioral characteristic of normalcy. (Note the last word. The double entendre is irresistible.)

COMMITMENT TO HONESTY

Honesty is supposed to rule the world in which I live—the fellowship of the church, the camaraderie of ministers, the changing contents of ministries. For a long time, I knew better. Consider: The primary spokesperson for the missions organizations in a local church frequently lectured members of the congregation regarding their lack of commitment to the gospel. At the same time, she provoked hostility among her associates by asserting judgmental superiority, offended visitors by condemning those who were different in order to elevate those whom she approved, and encouraged divisiveness by adamantly declaring her opposition to the inclusion of members of certain races in her community of faith. Really! A finance committee member counsels the pastor, "We are not concerned with numerical growth in this church. Don't feel any pressure in that regard. We just want to be a good church." Then, during the next period of preparation for the development of the annual budget, this same person addresses committee members saying, "We are just not growing. We must face that fact and hold the line on all accounts. We need to take a hard look at what or who is to blame for this situation." Ugh! A fellow minister in the community kindly passes along some pertinent information: "I'm going after some of your church members. Your theology is deplorable and your ministry is not very helpful. Now, please understand, I love you. I really do. But, I just can't sit by and be silent about my disapproval. I must provide authentic ministry for these people." Come on! After a heated discussion regarding a church's involvement in programs of rehabilitation for drug addicts, prisoners who have been paroled, and unwed mothers, the sentiment adopted by a majority vote affirmed an uneasy belief in the gospel of inclusiveness and redemption but acknowledged a respect for the congregation's right to abstain from controversial forms of ministry and enjoy a fellowship characterized by exclusion. Oh?

In the hospital, among colleagues in distress, I discovered a brand of honesty that is an enviable possibility for persons in ministry, for committees in any church. No facade was constructed to disguise personal opinions as biblical principles. Anger came unadorned. No double-talk was employed to create a perception that expressions of cold and calculat-

ing self-will were in reality revelations of God's will. Prejudice looked like prejudice. Rejection was unmistakable.
Emotions, words, and actions were all consistent with one
another.

"You look terrible. And I wish you would quit that
constant crying," one woman on edge spoke to another
woman almost over the edge. "Did you come in last night?" I
asked a new resident of the ward before breakfast one
morning. "Yes. I tried to commit suicide. But I feel much
better after a night's rest." During a group session, an older
woman says, "My son is soaking me for all I'm worth while
appealing to my love. Yet, I can't seem to let go." That stark
confession sparked a sudden assertion from a usually quiet
lady, "I no longer love my husband." In a conversation
between two people reported to be best of friends, one says
to the other, "You really screwed up!"

Listening to such comments, I could not help wondering,
Where are the intentionally distracting qualifications in
these remarks? Is there no attempt at subterfuge? Does this
woman not care how she sounds or how we will react to
what she is saying? Now I wonder, did I have to exit the
ecclesiastical realm and temporarily enter the domain of
emotional disturbances to discover honesty? I want to be
fair. Maybe the problem was with me alone. If so, I had
mastered the maintenance of it.

Over the years I have developed an incredible expertise in
deception. I can speak eloquently of emotions without being
emotional. Commendations become substitutes for what is
commended—emotional honesty, vulnerability, and intimacy. Numerous times in pressure-packed situations I have
handled intimidations adeptly with no revelation of fear. I
have listened to people praise my cool composure while my
heart threatened to pound its way out of my chest and my
stomach throbbed as it tried to dislodge a mass of knots.
Pains in the back of my neck were constant reminders that I
could not fool myself even if I fooled others. But that did not
stop me.

What part of this temperament was a perverted personal pride and what part a distorted professional image, I am not certain. In my mind, though, putting up a good front had something to do with being religious. Ministers are to be unflappable persons who are always in control. Besides, I had seen emotional abuse. I preferred the absence of emotions (as if that were really possible).

Distinguishing between cynicism and realism is not always easy for me. Cases in point are my responses to questions that inevitably arise when common problems seem to be subsumed under an uncommon piety. Compare a shabbily dressed woman in the hospital, whose face carries traces of the entrée from her previous meal, sitting sobbing and confessing, "I'm lonely and I need attention," and a very busy, sophisticated-sounding churchwoman who has just thrown a temper tantrum to get recognition for her services, while declaring, "I don't care if no one ever thanks me for what I do, I do it all for Jesus." Look at a heavily bearded man, whose calloused hands indicate his involvement in hard labor, checking into a hospital with an unrequested declaration of his problem, "I am mad as hell and someone is going to pay for it, even if it is me!" and a clean-cut professional fearful that any revelation of his anger will tarnish a much-admired spirituality, sitting in a church business meeting venting his thinly disguised wrath by criticizing the recent service of choral music and calling for the termination of a "lazy and uppity" custodian. These are the questions: Who is honest and who is not? Who is crazy and who is sane?

The honesty in my hospital ward was a wonderful discovery. So much pressure was removed by the realization that words did not have to be measured carefully so as to avoid bad impressions, that thoughts and feelings could be expressed straightforwardly without apologies, qualifications, and explanations. Speaking has more purposes than pleasing, helping, or impressing other people. A perfunctory "How are you?" can be answered with sincerity, "I am not

well today; I am sad," or "The joy within me feels like that of
a five-year-old on the way to her first circus."

Regardless of my identity as a minister, a friend, a casual
acquaintance, or a family member, I cannot expect other
people to be honest with me if I am not honest with them.
Honesty in words, deeds, and emotions is a necessity for
personal health as well as stability and growth in relationships. Such honesty relieves a great deal of inner stress as it
creates a most welcome freedom. I am learning the difference between laughter forced in search of social acceptance
(laughter which once quieted leaves one empty) and laughter that is an honest expression of the hilarious joy of
intimacy. Faking tears is as repulsive as it is wrong. Why
would believers in a church be less prone to practice
complete honesty than patients in a hospital?

MEANINGFUL RITUALS

Late on Friday evening, nearly three full days after I
entered the hospital, I called home. With excitement in my
voice, partially faked to be humorous but actually more real
than I ever will admit, I told Judy that I was the toughest
bingo player in the ward. Really. While playing bingo that
evening I had won two identical Christmas-tree ornaments
(at least one of which will always hang on our Christmas tree
as the most "expensive" ornament we own), two candy bars,
and a package of chewing gum. That is not much compared
to enjoying a seven-course meal in a five-star restaurant,
watching a professional basketball game at the coliseum, or
going to a symphony concert. But from where I was that
particular Friday night, playing bingo, let alone winning at
bingo, was a big deal. A bit of humor had broken through a
mood until now pervasively somber. Things would be severe
again, but for an important moment I had known levity.

Bingo was a Friday-night ritual for these folk. And a good
one. There were other rituals equally meaningful, though

not so noticeable. Bingo was an organized ritual. The others just evolved. Ask some of the patients there with me and likely they would not be aware of the ritualized nature of our various activities.

Matters taken for granted at home were subjects of special consideration in the hospital. Just after lunch on my first full day as a patient I learned that plans had been made for some people to leave the ward and walk around the campus. Hurriedly I went to the nurses' station to inquire about being a part of this excursion. My spirits sagged when I was told that I could not go along with this group because the staff did not yet know if I could be trusted. Never before had I been so disappointed about not getting to go outside. More positively, never before had the enjoyment of a leisurely walk in wintery air seemed so important.

Trust was a big deal. One of the rituals with which I was intrigued was mandated as a staff responsibility. Every ten to fifteen minutes, both night and day, a staff member had to verify the presence of every patient. Hospital personnel left no doubt that being—being there—was more important than doing. I suppose the constant-as-clockwork checking could have been resented. I saw it, though, as an interesting form of caring. Would that other institutions, including the church, were so committed to knowing the whereabouts of their people! For almost anyone, especially for someone who is depressed, sensing the importance of the repetitious census stands in sharp contrast to feelings (strong, even if wrong) that where I am is of little significance.

Intentionality so pervaded most hospital policies as to give them the nature of beneficial rites. Patients were not allowed to keep razors, hair dryers, radios, and other electrical appliances in their rooms. Therefore, a procedure was developed for requesting and returning these items, always with staff approval and assistance. Even a simple, habitual activity like shaving required preparation and became a reason for appreciation.

Eating was far from a perfunctory activity. Patients' preparations for meals became predictable. About ten minutes prior to each mealtime, three older women positioned themselves so they could see the doors that led into and out of the unit. While they talked nonchalantly, they gazed at those doors intently. When the cart of food trays was pushed through that entranceway, one woman, the same one every time, announced in a loud voice, "Here come the trays." (Her nerves were on edge if the delivery was tardy.) Word of the arrival of the food spread quickly. At the entrance to the dining room the younger patients unloaded the cart, placed the trays around the table, called out the person's name written on each tray, assisted, if needed, people to their respective places, and then removed the cover placed over each plate. It was an honor to be asked to help with the distribution of food.

For anyone accustomed to shoveling down a hamburger and french fries on the run and calling it lunch or sitting at the table during a "business luncheon" and having difficulty swallowing the ingredients of the salad because of the unnerving contents of the conversation ("I don't like the way things are going. Please pass the salt," a lunch partner says), hospital meals were real events. The food itself was discussed, maybe each item at a time. Comparisons of diets were unending. If the food was good, which was not always the case, every bite was savored. No one rushed. No external pressures prodded digestive problems. Mealtimes ended only as conversations waned and people decided to wander away. Good reasons existed to bow one's head and "return thanks" or "say a blessing."

Another particularly meaningful routine developed around saying good-byes. Life together for several days can result in relationships of some depth (bonding is strong in a fellowship of tears). No one going home just left the unit. At the last mealtime prior to a person's departure an announcement was made about the dismissal. Some cheered. Best wishes were offered. If plans for the days ahead had been discussed, efforts to carry out those plans were encouraged. Affirmations of support were sounded. Usually a few people applauded. Perhaps not everyone could verbalize the significance of this rite of passage, but instinctively people knew and recognized its importance.

My own departure from the unit was laughable as well as memorable. A recently admitted patient followed me to the nurses' station and watched the completion of the discharge procedures. Then, as my wife and I walked toward the exit, this woman repeated loudly, "When you get through that door, run! Run and don't ever come back." I was not sure I could run. But I knew my desire to not return here as a patient.

Driving home, I could not keep from thinking about the people I left behind and the rituals that would continue to fill their days. For every one of them I wished a speedy experience of the ritual of dismissal, though I suspected that for several that was not what they wanted—their rituals inside the unit constituted what they deemed to be a better life than the familiar routines of workplace and home.

Human scientists know well the value of routines and the wisdom of those who develop them. What does that say about my colleagues in distress? And what does that imply about all those whose activities go unaltered and pace unchanged in homes, offices, businesses, and churches where people succeed and fail, grieve and rejoice, go away and return, live and die? In retrospect, I am kind of proud of my multiple wins during Friday night bingo.

MUTUAL HELPFULNESS

In most mental-health units, at least one hour each morning and afternoon is devoted to group therapy. Everybody is expected, though not strictly mandated, to participate. Right away I could see the benefit of one type of the daily gatherings, at least in theory. Each session was organized around a major topic—stress reduction, time management, relaxation, and the like. A staff member made a presentation and served as a resource person. Discussion was encouraged. The format was familiar and thus attractive.

As it turned out, a sizable chasm separated the theoretical benefits of these sessions together from the actual results of these times. Leaders of the sessions dealt with materials that I had encountered early in graduate studies. Then, too, their mastery of the subject matter was at best intellectual, with a minimum of experiential insight.

A recall of my first two topic-oriented group sessions now produces a smile. The initial one was on anger and the second on depression. I was primed for each one, eager to receive help. Both experiences resulted in disappointment and the development of a dangerous attitude—"They can't help me." I left the session on anger angry, thinking, Why, I should have been the presenter. I know well firsthand what that staff person doesn't know very well secondhand."

Once more I wanted to establish my importance—to review curricula studied and seminars attended, to clarify my credentials. "After all, I am the helper—the teacher, preacher, counselor. Who did that young man think he was instructing me?" Fortunately, before acting foolishly (at least in this instance), I remembered that I was a patient and determined that I would get some good from each subsequent session. Those thoughts had to be processed more than once, but the result was beneficial participation in these groups.

Much more important was the second type of group session. The staff person present was mostly silent. Help during this hour was to be, derived by way of mutual assistance. Here again, my first response was rebellion. I could hardly believe the expectation—mutual assistance. Look who is present, I thought. What kind of comedy is this? These people can't help me. They don't know the pressures I face. They can't appreciate the problems I must solve. How is a woman with barely a sixth-grade education going to assist me? I have a graduate degree. How is a man who boastfully debunks religion to be helpful to one for whom religion is a matter of conviction and profession?

For my first hour in such a group, I sat down with my mind closed almost as tightly as my legs were crossed and my arms folded against my chest (the body language was a shout). But all of that changed.

Each group meeting began with a volunteer introducing the purpose and the ground rules for the time together. "This time is for us. We are encouraged to share with each other our thoughts, feelings, problems, and difficulties. We want to help each other. Remember, every word spoken in here is absolutely confidential. We are not to talk about other people's situations outside this room." The opening got my attention. At that moment and several times since, I have thought of what an appropriate statement that would be at the beginning of a Sunday-school-class session, a prayer meeting, or a ministers' gathering. "We are here to talk with each other for purposes of help, not to talk about each other as subjects of gossip."

Scanning the group-therapy participants, I saw genuine concern on people's faces. Even those who did not want to open themselves to sharing their problems and receiving help were interested in offering help to others. Compassion prevailed. Soon I found myself sharing seldom-spoken thoughts with people whose last names I did not know and listening intently to the counsel of people whose only credentials were an understanding of hurt and a desire to help. Good practical advice came from a woman whose broken words and poor grammar revealed her lack of formal education. Beneficial counsel regarding emotional integrity was offered by a young man whose wrinkled clothes were riddled with holes.

This image composed of mutuality and assistance, mutual

helpfulness, fascinated me. Who is an expert, anyway? How do you identify superiority in relation to a particular subject? Who knows better about coping with pain than people experiencing pain? Oh, sure, I have not lost sight of the value of advanced education, carefully researched information, and counsel derived from persons who have transcended a problem. But, as a minister, I recognize in the hospital therapy group an enviable spiritual model for community.

The claim of being an expert in matters of religion may be the best evidence to the contrary. Christian witness has been described as one beggar telling another beggar where to find bread. That is the image of group therapy—hurting people telling one another how and where to find help. And what of church groups? Can they ever be more than one problem-plagued sinner telling another about salvation and freedom and then waiting for the other to tell her something she needs to hear or to offer her something she needs to receive?

Mutual helpfulness among patients within a ward is good psychology. It isn't bad Christianity either. We can learn from one another, serve and be served. Undoubtedly, the apostle Paul's recognition of this truth lay behind his admonition for Christians to bear each other's burdens and share each other's sorrows as well as joys. Unfortunately, I had incorporated only part of this truth into my life. I am thankful for the ability now to see the whole. I long had known how to be a helper. At long last I was learning how to be helped.

My seven days' stay in the hospital was life-altering in the most positive sense. Precisely why, I do not know. No one event stands out in my mind as a "turning point" or a dramatic breakthrough. Excellent conversations with several different therapists were helpful. Dialogue in the group sessions was enjoyable. Extended quiet times for reflection brought a much-needed clarification of priorities, loyalties, values, and plans. In other words, benefit came from the gestalt—the whole period of hospitalization, everything put together, the totality of the experience formed from a variety of individual parts.

For me the hospital was a refuge—a place of retreat, rest, acceptance, comfort, counsel, healing, and resolve. I checked in on my way down, and I checked out having begun to climb back up. I departed from that hospital ward with insights, feelings, and intentions that I did not possess when I entered. For the first time in years I had a sense that healing had begun and a recovery of good health was possible.

Oh, yes, for many reasons, as did others, I feared getting out. But I knew I did not want to remain confined. I was ready to get on with my life, a better quality of life than I had experienced in a long time. I could anticipate that improvement not because of what stood before me or existed around me but because of what now was within me.

My neighbors in the mental-health unit were significant factors in the positive nature of my experience there. I am grateful for them. Did these folks constitute an unusual group at a special time? I doubt it. Very likely the dynamics of that unit are fairly constant. But the people I encountered there were helpful to me—their acceptance, tolerance, honesty, rituals, and helpfulness (maybe the better word is "ministry").

Looking back to those days of hospitalization, I am well aware of observing emotions in extreme states, abnormal behavioral patterns, drug-induced coping abilities, and words and deeds so unusual as to be laughable among the patients. But looking around, I see similar sights throughout supposedly more "normal" communities. Not seeking to glamorize an unglamorous experience or to describe in grandiose terms rather common developments, I can honestly say that I saw signs of health and principles of behavior among the people behind that locked door which, if embraced by people on the other side, could contribute to the enhancement of life in an open society. Now, sometimes playfully and sometimes seriously, I wonder if that magnetic door in the hospital really separated the normal from the abnormal, sickness from health, and more sanity from less sanity. Supposing it did; then I ask the more important question, Which side was which? Was the greater concentration of sanity outside the door or behind it?

4
When It Is Better to Receive Than to Give

Lessons learned early in life can linger as major influences later in life, regardless of their applicability and validity in certain settings. A rather innocent maxim which represents a simple truth in one context can exist as harmful counsel in another, more complex, situation. When such is the case, problems can develop and worsen in a person's life with no perception of what is wrong. As obedience to an unexamined teaching is continued, often with a discipline that is thought to be admirable, destructive forces are set in motion that promise serious trouble.

"It is more blessed to give than to receive." When I first heard those words, I have no idea. But I heard them repeatedly. The observation or admonition was conveyed with religious conviction, though for a long time I was not sure whether the words were a part of the biblical revelation. Like any child, I questioned the matter, thinking, It sure does seem like more fun to get gifts than to give them. But the platitude pointed to being "blessed," not "having fun." Thoughts continued: This must be one of those spiritual principles which will make more sense when I am an adult. Even if not, it is a moral rule which I must learn to follow. I bought the idea completely, eventually quit ever considering it quizzically, and finally found it to be true for me personally. Greater satisfaction accompanies giving than receiving.

Why? Why is that principle true? Please, I know the lecture "It's true because the Bible says it." I realize that the writer in Acts 20:35 attributes the words to Jesus. But a question is in order about the truth of the axiom in all areas of a person's life—my life specifically. Why do I get pleasure out of giving to others? Because I am obeying a teaching of the Bible? Perhaps, at least in part. Could it be a dimension of my compulsion to please other people? No doubt. Maybe I want affirmation from the recipient—"You are so thoughtful" (substitute "nice," "generous," or "caring"). Is it a kind of boomerang beneficence in which my gift is actually supposed to establish how wonderful I am more than to convey how important, how valuable, or how loved the other person is? If so, no need to worry. This form of selfishness looks just like goodness and passes for it almost daily.

Multiple explanations of the pleasure derived from giving, like mixed motives behind the act of giving, would not be unusual. But back to the original statement as a general principle of truth. After I wholeheartedly embraced the blessedness of giving, I did not stop to examine it critically. "It is more blessed to give than to receive." That's that. No attention was devoted to questions such as: Is that principle always true? What if I am depleted, practically devoid of anything to give? What is to be done when the dominance of unmet needs has virtually obliterated one's resources? What if ceaseless giving is causing a severe deterioration of health? How does this statement from Jesus relate to his emphasis on self-love? A consideration of these inquiries was not required because no questions at all were ever raised in my mind. "You know what the Bible says, 'It is more blessed to give than to receive.'" Thus, give. Give and be blessed.

Any general good commended to everyone tends to become a nonnegotiable goal commanded to ministers (who are supposed to be superior models in all realms of moral excellence). Giving of one's self and one's resources is made the very essence of ministering. Thus the comments: "My time is not my own. I can't even take a vacation. Sure, I would like to read and study more, but the press of people wanting appointments with me keeps my schedule full." To take a day off when "someone needs me" is interpreted as selfishness. To take the phone off the hook at dinnertime so the family can enjoy at least one meal a week without interruptions is deemed insensitive. Continuing education is considered a luxury. Tragically, such reasoning is often praised by supposedly supportive friends rather than challenged, with correction encouraged in love.

Endless giving is an impossibility for anyone without the infinite resources of God. To kid oneself at this point is to flirt with disaster (and to risk idolatry). As absurd as it seems when viewed objectively, here is a major problem in the ministry which, disclaimers aside, I knew personally.

CONFRONTING THE MESSIANIC COMPLEX

Many ministers could benefit greatly from regular visits by inquisitors such as those dispatched to Jesus by John the Baptist. The essential question of these emissaries from the imprisoned forerunner of the Messiah is crucial for our salvation, physically and emotionally as well as spiritually. "Are you the one?" That is, "Are you the Messiah?" John the Baptist and his followers did not think Jesus acted like the Messiah. Ironically, many who quickly and piously disdain the very thought of such a divine identity ("How ridiculous! How could you ever make such an inquiry?") give themselves enthusiastically to a messianic form of ministry.

Evidence of a "messianic consciousness" resides more in implicit assumptions than explicit intentions. Never did I, or would I, openly declare, "I will serve as the Messiah." But my actions revealed a "messianic mind-set." Observers of my work would have been justified in drawing the conclusion that my thinking contained certain presuppositions (though I would have categorically denied the reality of each one): I must help everybody in need. I am the only one who can minister effectively to most of these people; they want to see me, not someone else. I do not really have to have time for my family and myself. Serving is my purpose in living. If I don't take on more assignments, the important work of the church will not get done. I will respond positively to everyone who requests time with me. I must accept this one more speaking engagement; no one else can address this issue quite so effectively as I can.

Despite protests to the contrary (from this vantage point, it all sounds so sick), if I really did not harbor those thoughts, I unquestionably lived as if those were my thoughts. Who but the Messiah sees herself as indispensable in every ministry of the church, imagines that he never requires relaxation and rest, insists on being present at every meeting within a fellowship, determines to give leadership in all realms of an institution's life, always wants another challenge, refuses to acknowledge limitations, gives no thought to the needs of herself? Actually, no one, not even the Messiah. Jesus understood the importance of withdrawal for strength-replenishing privacy as well as commitment to demanding public ministry, of occasions for life-giving fellowship with friends as well as draining engagements with persons at their extremities, and of regular unrushed periods for recreative thought and prayer as well as long stretches of ceaseless preaching, teaching, and healing.

Among the many problems related to uninterrupted activity are a critical loss of reality concerning self-identity and the predictable accompaniment of a harmful diminishment of personal resources. I know of no one who consciously would tolerate even a hint of messianic pretensions. But such basic wisdom does not prevent an often subtle erosion of realism which allows for the justification of Godlike efforts to do the impossible. Motivated by genuine care but addled by an ever-increasing abundance of needs, delighted by the adulation of persons who have been helped and dazed by fatigue, ministers can forget their humanity completely and hurt themselves (and sometimes others) severely. An overinflated sense of self-importance is indicative of a dangerous, developing sickness. Efforts to do more and more are met with abilities to do less and less.

Once I had completed three days of psychiatric testing while in the hospital, a number of physiological examinations, including a CAT scan, were administered. I did not understand. When I asked my doctor for an explanation, his answer frightened me beyond description. The results of the psychiatric tests revealed a major problem. My test scores related to comprehension skills were far above normal. At the same time, the tests documented a serious weakness in my cognitive abilities. My capacity for making good decisions was virtually nil. The doctor explained that such a dramatic incongruity between comprehension and cognitive skills in a person usually is indicative of either a brain tumor, the inception of a mind-debilitating disease, or unresolved, long-term depression. The exact nature of my condition needed clarification.

I am thankful (what a strange place for a word of gratitude) to say that the composite results of the physical and psychological tests suggested that my problem was unresolved, long-term depression. I was relieved and disturbed. My relief had its source in anticipation—depression can be treated successfully and life resumed normally. My disturbance was rooted in reflection—I had been seeking to make major decisions without the ability even to handle minor concerns. Imagine the magnitude of the negative, even destructive implications of that situation.

Now here is the bitter irony (as well as the frightful severity) of the matter. At the very time I was most driven by a "messianic consciousness," not only was I devoid of the superior decision-making abilities of a messiah, I was without the capacities for discernment possessed by a normal human being. Even in brief moments of insight, when my comprehension of a situation prompted the conclusion "Something must change. You have to get help," I could not make a decision to act on that realization. Some messiah, eh? But no one is completely immune to such developments. And especially at risk are those persons so busy attending to the needs of others that they are not even aware of their own needs.

Sincere attempts to serve the Messiah give evidence of a virtue pleasing to God. However, all attempts—sincere, superficial, or whatever—to serve as the Messiah represent sins that are abhorrent to God. Like other sins, these actions can adversely affect a person's total health to such an extent that the need for help is hardly even recognized ("I'm all right. I just need to finish helping all the folks who need me today"), much less confessed so that assistance can be requested.

LEARNING TO ASK FOR HELP

A macho mentality existed in the church long before that word emerged and was popularized in society. Myths of self-sufficiency for any situation and assumptions of a comprehensive adequacy to face any difficulty were passed off as the strong benefits of a healthy spirituality. Supposedly, nothing was wrong with anyone that could not be corrected by "getting right with God."

Much of my life has been lived among persons who were almost offended by confessions of need, and so studiously silent regarding any kind of request for assistance. Images of strength and supposed evidences of spirituality were at stake. Couples would not participate in a marriage enrichment conference because their very involvement might suggest a weakness or a need in their relationship. Admissions of struggle were considered ugly tarnishes on faith.

Few would admit a problem to their pastor, and virtually no one would seek benefits from a professional counselor. Only with great hesitancy did many people even visit a medical doctor. Often persons who did seek help, for almost anything, were labeled as "crybabies" in need of a security blanket or freeloaders looking for a handout.

I bought it, this incredible idiocy. Or at least the idea possessed me. What is incumbent upon any Christian must be even more profoundly important for a Christian minister, I surmised. Strength. Sufficiency. No chink in the armor, no reason to reach for help. Amazing.

With the passing of time, I saw the truth in relation to others. Just like anyone else, Christians have needs that require help. Christian marriages get in trouble. Committed church persons face major problems. In fact, in sermons as well as informally, I encouraged parishioners to admit their needs and ask for help. But my counsel to others was not applicable to myself. Until later.

I grew very weary of being strong. Though I was dangerously slow in dealing with depression specifically, I knew something was wrong generally. Yet I could not admit that to anyone else. Thoughts of seeking help and laying out before another person my most private concerns were nauseating. I had this image to protect. "A good minister would not require such ministry from someone else," I kept telling myself, foolishly.

"What you are doing is not good. . . . The [task] is too heavy for you" (Ex. 18:17-18). These ancient words of Jethro directed to Moses conveyed the contemporary Word of God to me. And there was more: "I do have faith, but not enough. Help me have more!" (Mark 9:24, TEV). That confession of incompleteness and need elicited an implicit commendation from Jesus. When a Canaanite woman approached Jesus and without reservation stated, "Help me, sir!" Jesus responded by saying, "You are a woman of great faith!" (Matt. 15:25, 28, TEV). Great faith? My question about this text was followed quickly by a question about life. "Is there no inconsistency between living by faith, recognizing a need, and asking for help?" The Word of God was working on me.

Long before the most crippling depression appeared in my life, I had discussed from a pulpit how learning to ask for help is evidence of growth toward Christian maturity. Self-understanding is impossible apart from a recognition of one's need for assistance, and self-understanding is essential for meaningful living. As in so many other instances, here again the truth was in my head but not my heart. My mask of self-sufficiency did not come off easily. Nor did the hardened shell around my deepest emotions crack quickly. Even in the hospital, much later, during conversations with various therapists, I had difficulty coming completely clean about my needs. Finally, though, what I had known within myself I was able to say aloud, regardless of who overheard: "I need help." And, to a doctor, "Will you please help me?"

Progress toward the resolution of any serious problem is impossible until a need is admitted and help is requested. That truth is without exception regardless of one's vocation, trouble, or faith.

BEING SELFISH, OR
CARING FOR ONESELF?

How do you take care of yourself without practicing selfishness? That was a big question for me. Lifelong warnings from multiple sources blasted self-centeredness and selfishness as major sins, the epitome of evil. I did not want that. Even if I felt selfish, I did not want to appear selfish. But I knew I had to alter some of my daily habits and devote at least minimal attention to my personal needs.

The question that heads this section became almost a preoccupation for me in the first few days of my hospitalization. What is the difference between being selfish and caring for oneself? I was surrounded by competent professionals whose questions and suggestions were dominated by words and attitudes that sounded like what I previously had tried to avoid. "What do you feel? Why should you care what anyone else thinks of you? Give yourself the right to be selfish. Do what you need to do. At least for now, do not think of others."

Immediately I recoiled from such talk. They are dwelling on recommendations about which I have received considerable warnings, I protested to myself. (Never had I been told not to be concerned about what other people thought of me. The very suggestion sounded far too liberating to possibly be true.) Besides, in the hospital I saw people all around me whom I figured I could help (go ahead and laugh if you must). Fortunately, though, in time I decided that since they were the doctors and I was the patient, I needed to follow their instructions and wait until later to try to answer any questions I had about their advice. Progress.

A moment arrived (though I cannot pinpoint it precisely) when I resolved to devote all my attention to myself and to getting better. I was at peace with that plan (and fairly certain that it was consistent with the kind of self-love, which is distinct from selfishness, that is commended in the Bible). My intention was tested quickly.

Before anyone in the ward knew I was a minister, I avoided giving a direct answer to a man's question about my profession. Already he was seeking advice that I was incapable of offering. Later, after I was identified as a minister in a therapy group, an elderly woman came to me for counsel. She gently massaged my ego, explaining that she did not want to talk with the hospital therapists about her problems but that she trusted me. I almost took the bait, the same kind I have swallowed countless times before. But I caught myself just before putting on my "pastor's hat." I explained that I was there because I needed help myself and that she would do best to consult with her doctor.

Why could I not do that outside the hospital, before I came

here? I quizzed myself. More and more I came to regret that sensible acts of self-preservation had been considered selfish expressions of avoidable evil. Of course, responsible self-love is a spiritual principle. How could I have been so blind? Spiritually I wondered, If I do not take care of myself, do I not practice an irresponsible stewardship of God's gifts? Practically, I suspected, If I cannot take care of myself, I cannot hope to help take care of others.

The establishment of good habits of work and rest, the enforcement of preventive care, and attempts to maintain good health—these too are matters of morality which if violated result in a wrong every bit as bad as selfishness. Taking care of oneself is a responsibility by no means to be confined to the very worst moments of an illness or to a stay in a hospital.

A TIME FOR HEALING

The author of the Old Testament book Ecclesiastes was as cynical as he was helpful, wrong about as much as he was right. Running throughout his work is a refrain of pessimism born out of an obsession with predestination and a conviction that not anything would turn out right. Though Koheleth (a name capable of driving anyone to negativism and fortunately rendered "the Preacher" in our translations) categorized life too neatly and segmented time too narrowly, he did offer beneficial counsel regarding special experiences (or purposes) for unique moments. Set in the context of the larger biblical revelation, Koheleth's observation that there is a time for almost everything under the sun needs the complementary conclusion that never should any times be devoid of love, mending, reconciliation, making peace, and healing. However, the importance of unique moments is not to be missed. Ecclesiastes helps us to focus on that truth. For whatever reasons, a season can come with an agenda that dictates its most accurate designation and most correct utilization as that of "a time to heal."

My time for healing arrived apart from any preparation for its advent and any anticipation of how best to benefit from it. Good doctors, a wise wife, and two or three close friends offered helpful advice. Also, an insight from the ministry of Jesus has proven beneficial.

"Do you want to get well?" Posing that question to a sick person strikes me as cruel. Not an exemption from that judgment was my first reaction to Jesus' interrogation of a lame man at the pool of Bethzatha (John 5:1-9, TEV). For thirty-eight years this poor man had longed to experience the healing of those troubled waters. However, caught between reflections only of regret and the anticipation of no change, he remained crippled. As usual, the words of Jesus, even as insensitive as they seem at first, are tremendously insightful and helpful. Healing involves both the mind and the spirit—coming to a correct understanding and a decisive exercising of the will.

Faced with an undefined stretch of time with no professional responsibilities, I did not know what to do. Unfortunately, I fell back on the way of life I knew best and sought to apply it to this unfamiliar situation. Writing projects were outlined. Notations were made about books that I needed to read. Lists were made of people to write and phone calls to make. Goals were set with deadlines for making certain decisions and completing various actions. I thought I was doing all the right things until I was helped toward the understanding that doing was a big part of my problem.

I like recommendations, prescriptions, and directions that clearly define what needs to be done. I knew what to do about my hypertension—alter my diet, exercise, check my blood pressure daily, and take medicine. But I had no idea of what to do about depression, with its grief that required attention, guilt that demanded resolution, hurts that ached for healing, tension in need of relaxation, anger to be resolved, and self-esteem needful of reconstruction.

Illnesses of the spirit are not healed in the same manner as diseases of the body. A lack of understanding of this fact can be extremely harmful. For a while, I tried to treat a heartache like a headache, and disturbed emotions the same as an upset stomach. Obviously, I was not even addressing what was wrong, much less pointing myself in a direction that was right.

Understanding is essential in a time for healing. Some sadness cannot be removed by exchanging funny jokes. Not all forms of loneliness are alleviated by the presence of people. Guilt can remain after the forgiveness of God has been declared. Fear may not be destroyed by the installation of night-lights and burglar alarms. Insecurity often prevails despite prospects for a job with financial income. Trust is not easily or quickly reinstated.

Most important for me were, first, understanding what was wrong and, second, understanding that both the present and the immediate future constituted a time for healing—healing, nothing else. Significant improvement began when I released myself from the obligation to return every phone call, to answer every letter, to stop by my former office to pick up the mail, to find out what was going on in my denomination, to chase down every rumor and attempt to correct what was false, to check up on former counselees, to portray a picture of steady improvement. This was a time for healing.

Time was needed for professional therapy and informal chats with friends, talking seriously with my wife and sons, and sometimes avoiding deliberately any subject that was remotely serious, reading a book because I wanted to rather than needed to, or watching a movie, sometimes the same one more than once. Regularly moments were claimed for complete silence. Satisfaction came in allowing tears to flow and laughs to erupt. Understanding!

Healing is also a matter of the will. Jesus knew what he was doing when he asked the lame man, "Do you want to be healed?" I did. I do. Feelings of quitting everything and just giving up completely, present for a long period of time, subsided during my stay in the hospital. I found a new drive toward meaning, fulfillment, ministry, and joy. I willed to be well. But I had no desire to rush into anything. My will to be well necessitated a time of healing. The two were inseparably related. I gladly gave myself to such a time.

Though I had read the writings of Viktor Frankl much earlier, I now understood his invaluable insights better than ever before. A "will to live" is of fundamental importance. With it, difficult situations and disorders can be overcome. Without it, people can die of diseases that have simple cures. My will to live dictated complete commitment to a time of healing.

For the first time in my life I realized that I was in a situation in which it was better to receive than to give. And I sensed that my attitude was not wrong and that I was not alone. I was learning a new dimension of the love of God.

5
Healing Hurts

Well before I left the hospital, I wanted the doctor to answer a nagging question: "Do you think I can function as a minister again?" At that time, hearing someone else's opinion—especially, from a doctor, the positive one which I heard—was very important to me. Later, though, I became more concerned with my own response to that inquiry. Fortunately, clarity on that issue has prevailed. The product of months of careful introspection, reflection, and anticipation is a staunch conviction that I am better prepared to function effectively as a minister at this point in my life than at any previous time.

Still a problem, though, is an anxiety-laden uncertainty. Will any congregation or institution give me a chance to serve as a minister again? What if prospective employers are afraid of me because of the previous hypertension and/or depression? Will a lengthy bout with a destructive disorder cause me to qualify for that category of "a poor health risk"? Worse still, what if any of the innumerable rumors about me have been accepted uncritically and made future ministry a virtual impossibility? Great frustration develops from the realization that the very hurt that could disqualify me from ministry in the minds of some people is a tremendously enabling factor in an enhanced competency to do ministry among all people.

After enduring a period of subjection to battering questions, disturbing doubts, and draining considerations of other possibilities, I know I am a minister. That identity is independent of any institutional position, specific professional possibility, or other person's (or persons') opinion. Functioning as a minister has legitimacy apart from the source of one's salary. My ministry holds more promise than ever before in terms of a capacity to address profound human concerns and to help people who hurt. My own hurts serve as important sources for ministerial acts of healing.

A brief fictional sketch from Thornton Wilder is loaded with special truth. Present and past are united against a backdrop of the biblical narrative found in the fifth chapter of the Fourth Gospel. A busy physician is plagued by a personal wound which he cannot heal. This troubled man makes his way to the infamous pool at Bethzatha, hoping to dash into the churning waters and find healing. According to tradition only the first person to enter the waters after they begin to stir benefits from their healing properties.

As the eager physician waits, carefully watching the waters so as to detect the slightest indication of their movement, an angel appears beside him. This heavenly being urges the doctor to withdraw from the pool, observing that healing is not for him. The angel explains that the doctor's wound is the source of his power. After hearing how one broken human being is more persuasive with other hurting people than even a heavenly band of angels, the doctor is told that in the service of love, only wounded soldiers can serve.

Tremendously disappointed, the physician turns away from the now bubbling waters of the pool and heads home. As he moves along, he is met by the man who jumped into the healing waters in front of him. This newly healed fellow has come to plead with the doctor to come to his house for one hour so as to help his son, who is overcome with dark thoughts. Confessing that he cannot even understand his son, the father speaks of his certainty about the physician's ability to help. Memory is activated, and suddenly the doctor understands the meaning and significance of the angel's declaration that in the service of love only wounded soldiers can serve.

Isn't that just a neat rationalization for someone in a bad situation? a cynic could ask. Is it? I want to know. Am I only trying to give the best possible interpretation to a not-so-good situation, to throw all the positive light available on a period of darkness? Is this thing about wounds that heal, hurts that help, just so much wishful thinking?

Once again I have been made aware of the saving quality of the Scriptures. Isaiah's description of the ministry of the Suffering Servant includes the assertion, "With his stripes we are healed" (53:5). Jesus made no effort to separate problems and pain from ministry. His guest list of persons invited to the party made analogous to God's Realm would be humorous if the subject were not such a serious one. Summoned ahead of anyone else were the lame, the deaf, the blind, the hated, the oppressed, tax collectors, prostitutes, adulterers, and thieves. Paul, the apostle, made a stunning statement about his gratitude for insults, hardships, calamities, and persecution, claiming them as prerequisites for his confession, "For when I am weak, then I am strong" (2 Cor. 12:10).

Henri Nouwen's well-known picture of the positive power of a wounded healer comes straight from Holy Scripture. The truth of related biblical narratives is duplicated repeatedly in personal experiences. Properly handled, hurts to oneself bear the promise of help to others.

CLARIFICATION OF IDENTITY

I am scared of a person who has never hurt. Individuals who have known only health, success, and happiness typically are insensitive to sickness, failure, and sadness as well as intolerant of people plagued with those maladies. Such untouched-by-pain persons can pass harsh judgments upon others without hesitation and even, with no reservations, head up holy crusades to obliterate all signs of weakness and sin in institutions, events, or individuals. I fear such individuals so mightily because I have met so many of them personally, and I know their tendencies even as I know their names.

People who boast that no wrong ever will overtake them, no problem ever shake them, or no weakness ever aggravate them possess severely distorted self-images. (The very existence of such individuals seems like an impossibility theoretically, though in actuality they are encountered all too frequently.) Instead of a praiseworthy faith, such statements exhibit a poor understanding of the complex makeup of human nature and the infinite compassion of the divine nature. Problematic for people who cultivate this mentality is permission for persons to be human and for God to be God.

Only in hurting do many of us (if not all of us) find out what life is really like. To be oblivious to the essential nature and meaning of existence is tragic itself—to be unfamiliar with disappointed hopes and unrealized dreams, insensitive to physical aches and pains, without appreciation for the powerful truths that can emerge from dark nights of the soul. Similarly, only in hurting do some of us discover that we are finite creatures, not competitors with the infinite Creator; responsible persons capable of failure, not mechanical robots programmed only for success; sinners with the capacity to perpetrate horrible evils, not perfectionists with possibilities only for good; confessors constantly in need of forgiveness, not judges impatient with guilt; seekers looking for redemption, not self-appointed messiahs working out our own salvation. If occasionally I flex my muscles and imagine myself to be the master of my fate, the captain of the world and my own soul as well (though I must admit that such musings have not been present for months, or even years), most days I know better, acknowledging my need for the compassionate guidance of God and the sympathetic fellowship of neighbors.

Hurt can clarify identity, though this doesn't always happen. In the midst of pain, failure, sin, and suffering people can see themselves and know themselves as never before—integral parts of the creation which groans for salvation, members of a community of redemption which confesses sins, pleads for forgiveness, and reaches out for hope. In reality, apart from such an understanding of life, most of us will not even admit hurt, much less accept hurting as a potential means for healing.

MATURATION OF COMPASSION

People who have not hurt do not know (probably cannot know) the true nature of love. Even the world with all its folly understands that reality and can spot a phony lover a mile away. To pledge love while exhibiting no vulnerability and demonstrating no sensitivity is to reveal a deception of oneself. Few, if any, will be convinced that mature compassion is present.

As a minister, I have been haunted by two of Emerson's entries into his journal after listening to sermons. In the first instance, the noted author observed that the man who spoke from the pulpit gave no evidence of ever having lived at all. Listeners received no indication that the preacher had cried or laughed, loved or married, been affirmed, cheated, or slandered. The man's message seemed devoid of truth because it was divorced from life.

In the second instance, Emerson registered his impatience and hostility toward the preacher whom he just had heard drone on and on about consolation and joy before a congregation of people preoccupied with calamity. The speaker's neatly organized sermon stood in sharp contrast to the disarray of his listeners' lives. Emerson had had it. He wanted this preacher silenced. No real sense of compassion for the minister was felt, because no indication of his familiarity with hurt was conveyed. (God deliver me from such a personal and homiletical debacle, I pray even as I write these words.)

Few people will tolerate even the most carefully honed and eloquently spoken sermons about love (or most other subjects) unless they can see in the communicator an awareness of the hurt inherent in love when life is troubled. Actually, the crucial principle here is applicable to far more than preaching. Evangelism dictated by a prescribed formula and practiced according to a routinized technique, evangelism devoid of genuine pathos and compassion, will be ineffective. A mission accepted only as a job, duty, or obligation might as well be left alone. Interpersonal relationships sought by way of a guidebook filled with stylized comments and stereotyped expectations never will develop. Folks just are not convinced that they are loved unless they see a vulnerability to their hurts and the presence of a spontaneity that could explode in laughter or tears.

Mature love is unmistakable when people see in the lover a willingness to hurt because they hurt, an openness to sharing the burden of their pain. That, by the way, is not only true compassion, it is the only means of redemption.

CREATION OF IDENTIFICATION

I hate glib comments and deplore empty clichés. Perhaps the only thing worse is to be met in the midst of a difficult situation by a person who attempts to offer comfort by saying, "I understand," when a lack of understanding is blatantly obvious to all who see and hear. Helpfulness is found in the assertion "I understand" only when the speaker has known the hurt produced by a similar crisis. When that is the case, however, a true kinship in trouble is so readily recognizable that no words are necessary. Eyes meet and the message of empathetic love is delivered. The bonding that takes place in a fellowship of pain is incredible.

For much of my ministry I functioned primarily as a merchant of words. I know the right situation-dictated words to speak and I can state them reasonably well. But often words are inappropriate. Frequently, hurting people do not need to hear anything. Appendicitis is not eliminated with a scholarly review of surgical procedures developed to carry out an appendectomy. Lectures on headaches are not considered cures for hurting heads. Why, then, imagine that grief can be relieved by an explanation of sorrow or loneliness diminished by a lecture on friendship or guilt removed with a homily on righteousness?

The first step toward healing in the life of one who is hurting is a sense that the person offering help is not intimidated or threatened by the hurt but ready to be identified with the hurt and the one who is hurting. Personally, a prolonged agony produced within me a capacity for understanding a hurting individual and communicating silently to her—by way of body language, a glance, or a facial expression: "I know. And I am with you." No need exists to offer an explanation to the person, to pass judgment, or to make recommendations. Often help and healing follow. Establishing a fellowship of hurt is the prelude to realizing a fellowship of health and hope.

The operative dynamic here was obvious in the ministry of Jesus. People who have known betrayal, rejection, conflict, false charges, mistrials, and insensitive holiness were (and are) drawn powerfully to Christ because of their sense of his compassionate identification with them. As the hurts of Christ coincide with the hurts of scores of persons, an opportunity for healing is created.

Invariably, individuals in need will seek out other individuals who identify with their needs. Even a faint hint of accomplished perfection will frighten away the hurting. They are drawn toward people characterized by weakness and possessed of an acceptance of doubt, fear, hopelessness, failure, and sin. I know. As a person in need, I have sought help from people with an ability to identify with pain. Now, all too familiar with hurt, I want to be a helper to those in whom hurt persists.

CONTRIBUTION TO MINISTRY

A minister and her ministry cannot be the same after experiencing profound hurt. That principle is practically sound and scripturally persistent. More than one biblical commentator has identified the wounds of a person of God as sources of power in that person's ministry. Who better can help wounded people than one who has been wounded?

Several similar questions bear within themselves their important answers: Who better can offer fellowship than one who knows the trauma of alienation? Who better can speak of trust than one who has been betrayed? Who better can extend comfort than one who has borne grief? Who better can commend faith than one who has dealt with doubt? Who better can uphold truth than one who knows the destruction of deceit? Who better can ascend to heights of joy than one who has sunk to the depths of despair? Healing for some often comes by means of the hurts of others.

Grateful to God for an enhanced and highly sensitized ability to minister effectively in Christ's name, I still stop short of giving thanks for the painful experiences which are now credentials for such ministry. In retrospect (often a place of increased wisdom), I never would choose to travel the path that brought me here. I can take no credit for any new competence. After falling flat on my face, God helped me get up. In subsequent days, as I stumbled toward strength, God lifted my head, brightened my eyes, focused my thoughts, squared my shoulders, straightened my back, enlivened my steps, and equipped me for meaningful ministry.

Theology has become autobiography. Christianity is no guarantee of protection from problems, mistakes, pain, ill health, failure, hurt, and suffering. Not at all. Rather, in the face of such difficulties, Christianity is a powerful resource for coping. At work in the crucifixion and resurrection of Jesus was the power of God available to God's people always. Personalized, that means God can take the worst I offer (which is a source of divine displeasure) and transform it into a medium for good (which is a source of divine pleasure). Within Christianity, all kinds of problems, pains, hurts, suffering (including depression), and, yes, even acts of sinfulness are embraced by God, transformed, and returned to us as experiences that strengthen ministry, mediums that extend healing.

From despair can come hope. Out of pain, promise can grow. Cries for help can be replaced by offers of help. Weeping can give way to laughing. Wounds can become sources of healing. Thanks be to God!

6
Straight Talk:
Lessons for Living

"What did you learn from your experience?" always has been an important question for me. Repeatedly I have put that inquiry before persons returning from a sabbatical leave, recovering from a major physical illness, attempting to piece life back together after a shattering disappointment, reentering society after working through a period of prolonged grief, looking for a new job after a forced termination in the previous one, stating a desire to remarry after enduring the emotional battering of a bitter divorce, embarking on a new direction after long-term dreams have been pronounced dead. Now I must ask myself what I have asked others. I dare not be done with the bother of that self-interrogation until I lay hold of answers that augur well for the future.

Directive counsel is the substance of this chapter. Like the content of the rest of the book, this material initially was written for myself. I have an affinity for summations and conclusions. I need sharp-pointed discussions. Predictably, not all people share my propensities in this regard. Persons with a preference for nondirective dialogue, subtlety, and diagnoses of difficulties with no recommendations for their prevention or solution best bypass these pages.

No claim of unique competence or authoritative expertise

accompanies these words. Having endured a series of painful experiences and, at least to this point in time, not only survived but grown, probably constitutes my best credentials for writing anything at all. The thoughts that follow have been formed apart from any sense of having "arrived." They may be understood best as a report to all who journey, from a pilgrim somewhere along the way, a sojourner who prefers the risk of not being helpful at all to remaining silent about matters that could enable others to avoid a repetition of his mistakes, to minimize their own hurts, and to grasp important hints of hope.

ADVICE TO ADULTS

My first impulse was to address these words specifically to ministers. That would have been a mistake. The making of a minister is the making of a person. Besides, almost all adults face similar problems, confront predictable stresses, harbor habitual fears, and entertain common concerns. No one profession has a monopoly on value, meaning, and truth. Or on need. No one person is exempt from the potential to receive benefit from experienced counsel. So, for all who care to have a look, to risk reading several lines in order to find one helpful word, here goes.

Trust God alone. "Trust God" is an affirmation of the importance of the religious dimension of life generally and an assertion regarding the necessity of a constant reliance on the incomparable resourcefulness of God specifically. "Alone" is a qualifier meant to imply a warning.

"Trust God." That counsel needs no elaboration. Behind it are the weight of the biblical revelation, the strength of the truth evidenced in Christian history, and the testimonies of countless numbers of believers who have found in a redemptive relationship with God what is unavailable anywhere else. God is worthy of our worship, meriting our trust, and deserving of our faith. God alone.

No human being comes close to God's reliability and thus to the validity of God as the object of unconditional trust. To assign absolute attributes to any person is to lose sight of human limitations and to open oneself for disappointments and hurt. Actions oriented to the way things "ought to be" can result in devastation fostered by the way things "really are." Promises are broken. Friends fail at critical moments. Covenants are corrupted. Those who claim love bring harm. Disappointments destroy confidence.

Cynicism is not the foundation for these words. Realism is. Nothing vicious is operative here. Fear and self-preservation simply are powerful components of life. They can weaken the best of intentions and elicit undesirable actions. Given the proper circumstances, betrayal can look very moral. Frequently crises provoke a reversion to primitivism— "Don't worry about anyone else. It's everybody for herself." Though I believe strongly, I must also deal with practicality. For many people, pressure makes everything negotiable, causing the assertion, "All promises are off." Mental tricks can justify callous cruelty or insensitive meanness and make both look like admirable righteousness.

Remember that deception destroys more than it preserves. Ethicists write of the "law of the inclined plane." The principle is that one untruth requires another untruth which, in turn, requires another and then another and then another. Thus, deception sends life plummeting downhill. Believe me, the matter is not mere theory.

Motivations for deception often seem perfectly rational, justifiable, maybe even moral. In many instances no evil is intended. Deception can be practiced to maintain an image, to preserve the power of an office, to prevent loved ones from experiencing anxious concerns, to protect an institution, to avoid embarrassment, and to perpetuate proper public relations. Conveying untruth is not the issue so much as not telling all of the truth or simply covering up the truth.

Just as dishonesty destroys integrity morally, deception erodes stability emotionally and jeopardizes personality totally. Portraying an external image of strength and confidence while enduring an internal storm of fears, insecurities, and weakness takes a heavy toll on health. Laughing and smiling while repressing sobs and fighting back tears requires excessive expenditures of irreplaceable energy. Nodding agreeably and speaking pleasantly to persons who have incited anger and shoved nerves to the edge create a pain-causing tension difficult to relieve. Repeated responses of "Great" and "Just fine" to the question "How are you?" prod the development of knots in the stomach or the creation of nausea.

Significant among the many valuables lost through deception is self-respect. Disgust develops toward oneself and irrationally spills over toward almost everybody else. Usually anger follows close behind. Seeing no value in oneself, questions are raised about the possibility of any value at all. Relationships are ruptured. Work and worship are affected adversely. Life is reduced to chaos (at least internally, but if uncorrected, eventually externally as well).

Is it worth it just to look good and to sound good? So what if the exemplary professional image is preserved, but at a cost of the destruction of the person behind the mask? What is so wrong with being weak sometimes, not knowing all the answers, and admitting a need for assistance?

Count the cost. Everything comes with a price tag on it—tangibles and intangibles alike. Figuring costs is easy if the issue is what kind of house to live in, what style clothes to wear, and what model car to drive. Realities and possibilities are as clear as numerical bottom lines. Not so easy or clear, but every bit as much a necessity, is calculating the expenditures required for "making it" in one's profession, scaling the "social ladder," achieving the reputation of an expert, pleasing peers, and existing as a model church person. Is what is sought worth the price that must be paid to attain it?

Assessing costs is not only a matter of facing realities ("Do I have the resources required to meet this goal?" "I know I can begin this work, but do I have the assets to complete it?") but of deciding about values. Many acquaintances will be impressed by long hours of work, but what experiences will be missed in relation to those special people whom I love? Watching a child's first step, celebrating a sixteenth birthday, holding a spouse's hand in the surgical waiting room, and walking with a friend on his way to his daughter's wedding are nonrepeatable events. Each is either grasped at the moment pregnant with meaning or lost. Impressive notations on one's dossier can increase rapidly while joy and meaning in life dissipate almost entirely. Sometimes the satisfaction of being personally able to close every business deal pales in significance against the realization that physically fatigue is almost unbearable, emotionally an explosion is near, and relationally life is empty.

My concern is not so much whether a person can finish what is started or not, but what is lost in the process. What is given for what is gained? At stake in the answer to that question are health and happiness and so much more.

Costs accompany the embrace of positive values as well as of negative ones. To choose to live by love is to risk getting hurt. Deciding to be a disciple of Jesus involves freely taking on discipline. If openness and vulnerability are valued, getting taken advantage of or being misunderstood can be expected. Assertions of faith invite blasts of criticism. An elevation of grace may be condemned as a commendation of permissiveness. But these are the costs without which life would have little, if any, worth at all.

Do not ever say "never." Anyone who does not enjoy eating his own words will do well to heed this counsel. Absolute declarations such as "I will never do anything like that," "I will never allow myself to get in that kind of situation," and "My positive attitude will never change" spring from a woefully inadequate recognition of human possibilities and limitations.

Question almost any parent who has been through the maturation process of a child. Perfectionist plans for child-rearing are quickly revised as we relate to the special needs of a son or daughter, a mentality loaded with "nevers" giving way to the more flexible thought of "maybe" or the completely altered mind-set of "I guess it's all right, but I would not have believed I would ever consent to such a thing." Similar situations develop as newlyweds adjust to each other and settle into a life together.

Adamant assertions bordering on presumptions of perfection alarm me. Watch out for people who think they are too good, too disciplined, too faithful, too healthy, too courageous, or too wise to worry about certain problems in their lives. That disciple who, on the eve of the crucifixion of Jesus, backed up to a campfire in Jerusalem and denied any knowledge of the Messiah was the same stormy personality who only a few hours earlier, offended by Jesus' prediction of his betrayal, boisterously declared that he never would deny his Lord. Peter has plenty of spiritual kin. Often the louder the protests of "never," the harsher and more painful are the protesters' violations of their promises.

More times than I am comfortable counting, I have found myself speaking words, displaying attitudes, and tolerating actions that I had previously denounced as I had observed them in others and had resolved never to have anything to do with myself. Apologies seem weak. For such behavior I need forgiveness from both God and those people whom I first criticized and then emulated.

Recognizing every human's capacity for all sorts of sickness, failures, and evil nurtures a healthy humility, elicits an awareness of the importance of constant God-directed trust, stops self-righteousness cold, and creates a passion for minimizing being judgmental and maximizing mercy.

Be a friend. With the passing of years, a long-standing observation has grown into a staunch conviction: Everybody needs at least one friend. Experiences within time, however, not just time itself, contributed most to my elevation of the value of friendship. I have known the comfort derived from a companion who in difficult circumstances as well as occasions for joy served as a friend. Also, I have known the bitter disappointment (which quickly becomes excruciating pain) of apathy, neglect, betrayal, or even deliberate hurt from someone who was thought to be a friend.

Being aware of my own need for friendship has helped me to see friendship as a precious gift which I can share with someone else. Giving to assure getting is not the issue, though. Friendship does not work that way. The resolution to be a friend may result in a relationship with someone who does not know how to be a friend in return. That is all right.

Actions expressive of a friendship are no mystery: a supportive phone call just before a crucial meeting; an inconvenient visit for the sole purpose of communicating "I care"; sharing a crazy story at an unexpected moment; not only saying, "I will do anything I can to help," but meaning it and then acting on it; devoting a day to a no-agenda outing; listening to a painfully honest discussion of events and embracing every word with an unfailing confidentiality; making a big deal over an accomplishment and hosting a celebration of recognition; refusing to allow put-downs of a person to go unchallenged; dropping by to inquire, "Would you like to take a break and go for a ride?"; being as faithful and helpful when apart as you would appear to be when together.

One day the phone in my office rang. I picked up the receiver to hear a dear friend in another city say, "I know you are shoveling a lot of manure right now. I'm sorry. You are in my thoughts. I want you to know I love you. Good-bye." A bolt of comfort-giving, strength-encouraging compassion right out of the blue. How did she know? What prompted that call at just the right time? Those questions came immediately. But they quickly gave way to a serene enjoyment of a sense of warmth inside and tears on my face.

To be that kind of friend to someone is a worthy goal. Jesus equated sacrificial giving on behalf of a friend to experiencing the greatest love of which people are capable.

Play. You read it correctly. The "l" is not a misprint for an "r." To pray is important. But so is to play.

Words of caution on this subject seem inappropriate. But experience documents a tendency that needs to be addressed. Resolve to play. But be careful not to work at play so hard that the play becomes work. All too often a means of recreation develops into an emotions-disturbing obsession, a financially draining preoccupation, very nearly an alternative profession. Play intended to relieve the stress of work can become a new source of pressure.

Heeding my recommendation to play does not require taking any lessons, paying any fees, purchasing any equipment, or conforming to a dress code. Play may take place on the living room floor, on a vacant lot in the neighborhood, at the city park, or in the backyard.

Going to a circus qualifies, but so does rolling in fallen autumn leaves. Watching a hummingbird feed is just as good as joining a table game of some kind. The thrill of downhill snow skiing at a noted resort is great fun. But so is an all-out war between snowball throwers on the wintry battlefield of someone's unplowed front walkway. Jogging or walking to strengthen one's heart can be enjoyable as well as beneficial. Sometimes, though, discipline needs to be set aside for strolling about at a snail's pace or frolicking hilariously.

Let go and play. Play uninhibitedly. Play noisily. Allow pent-up pressures to find release in a breathtaking, energy-expending dash across a meadow brilliantly colored by wildflowers heralding the coming of spring. If you just cannot get away from concentration, study the beauty of a field of bluebonnets, concentrate on the variations of red in a single rose petal, or ponder the plight of a vivid black-and-yellow bumblebee working a garden of flowers to collect nectar. Do not hold back the expressions of joy that emerge from the depths. Perhaps easily understandable shouts of pleasure or loud laughs of happiness can replace (or make unnecessary) destructive screams of anger or eruptions of repulsive profanity.

Take care of yourself and your family. No one is going to watch out for the best interests of yourself and your family like you. Other people have a "thousand things" on their minds while trying to "stay above water" in their own pursuits. Often, the existing good intentions of others never reach fruition. No harm is intended and they are genuinely sorry, but they have to take care of "first things first."

Seldom will an employer (business, church, government) reprimand an employee for consistently working long hours to "stay on top of the job." To the contrary, employers and peers frequently support a person's senseless work habits by affirmation and praise: "I admire the way you can go for weeks without a day off. I wish I had your kind of discipline. We are so fortunate to have such a hard worker as you among us." The individual involved actually may feel worse and worse, though the adulatory comments convince him that he is doing better and better.

No superparent will show up to dictate directions: "You must get an annual physical checkup. Take your designated day off. Spend a regular evening with your family, or with your children so your spouse can get out. Plan a weekend retreat with your spouse. Do not schedule appointments on nights your daughter has a basketball game. Calendar a family vacation and commit yourself to those dates." God gave us minds to use in the service of good sense. At times we must say sternly to ourselves what we are unlikely to hear from others.

All kinds of people with all kinds of needs will claim every bit of the energy, time, and attention you will give them. If you do not put on the brakes periodically, say, "Enough," and take better care of yourself, they will accept the benefits of your efforts, shake their heads, and say, "It is his decision to be that way. I don't know how long he can last. But I guess he knows what he is doing."

Though people are prone to admire hard work, most people also appreciate individuals who take care of themselves and their families. But if self-caring or family-oriented acts are not even understood by anyone else, much less praised, the people who matter get the point, find help, and experience love.

Keep in touch with reality. "Oh, come on. Remember whom you are talking to!" The words of challenge come from a friend every time he hears me dodging facts or not confronting reality in some other manner. I listen, unappreciatively at first. A nervous laugh on my part follows. Then, I begin to speak again, cautiously trying to deal with matters as they are.

A minister friend, older than most persons still preaching, has an interesting practice. When he is to speak, knowing the problems that advanced age can cause in the mind, he invites people whose honesty is dependable to sit in the congregation, listen, and then give him feedback following the service. He asks his friends to evaluate the content and delivery of his sermon so that he will not lose touch with reality, fail to recognize it, and continue preaching after a time when he should have stopped. I admire this wise friend more than ever.

My fear is that most of us would just as soon deny reality as face it, particularly if we are not apt to like what we see. Warning signs are needed: CAUTION, DANGER. Flights from reality can be very destructive.

Good decisions are highly unlikely if a person is out of touch with reality. No possibility of improvement exists until there is an admission that something is wrong. Responsible plans for the future cannot be made apart from an accurate awareness of the present. Tragically, relationships can dissolve, effectiveness in work dissipate, health deteriorate, and a multitude of problems mount up in the absence of a keen sense of reality.

Help people to understand that you do not want to hear from them only what they think will not disturb you. Stress with others your need to know the truth. In your own thoughts, make yourself face reality as well, whether reading regular printed reports, learning from the body language of others, picking up on what is not said to you as well as on what is said, or polling for the opinions of people you trust.

Construction of a strong and meaningful life is impossible if the foundations for that life are more fanciful and imagined than real.

Ask for help. Admissions of a need for assistance can indicate admirable strength as well as wisdom. At some time or other, everyone needs help. Smart people ask for it. Those who remain silent often suffer needlessly.

Self-made and self-sufficient people are the projections of a myth every bit as problematic as it is popular. No such creatures exist. The noun and the adjective negate each other. The subject, "people," disqualifies the modifiers, "self-made" and "self-sufficient."

Guard against the confusion fomented by the mixed messages afloat in our culture. Enduring a worsening pain without seeking medical care is being stupid, not tough. Attempting to do alone tasks intended to be done only by many should not be considered courageous, aggressive, or industrious, but dumb. Taking on more than any one person can handle is deplorable rather than admirable. Defying physical limitations and crossing dangerous emotional boundaries even on behalf of good causes are much closer to sins in need of repentance than to a piety meriting praise or holiness worthy of emulation.

Spending time with a psychiatrist in an attempt to overcome depression is no more an indictment of one's religious faith than sitting in a dentist's chair requesting that a throbbing tooth's cavity be filled. Asking an associate for assistance on an assignment no more represents ineptness than requesting someone to help you lift a heavy piece of furniture. Inviting advice from others is every bit as important as offering advice to others.

Whether directed to others as a mark of professional ingenuity, to a physician as a realization of a need for medical attention, to a family member as an indication of intimacy, or to God as a sincere prayer of spiritual devotion, wise, powerful, life-changing words for anyone are, "Please, help me."

Keep the faith (or, allow the faith to keep you). The emphasis here falls on "being" rather than "doing." Actually, there is not much anyone can *do* about faith. The initiative is with God—the offer of acceptance in love, forgiveness by grace, sustenance with hope. Do not fight it like beating at water in an attempt to stay afloat. Relax and live in it, like leaning back on the water and floating with the support of an entire ocean. Faith in God is not a heavy burden to be carried. Rather, faith is most profound when we allow God to carry us. Accepting our acceptance—that is the way the great Paul Tillich put it.

Faith is not threatened by doubts, problems, illnesses, failures, and sins. Honesty in the face of faith is encouraged. Pretenses about perfection are unnecessary. A person of faith need not hesitate to declare, "I blew it," "I am frightened by the need for a biopsy," "I have sinned and enjoyed it," or "I feel as if I must question everything." Difficulties do not scare away God. No less a person of faith than the apostle Paul said rather matter-of-factly that nothing—nothing!—can separate us from the love of God (Rom. 8:31–39).

Persons who need to feel they have paid the proper price for a possession or lived so as to be worthy of a particular gift will have big problems here. What we have done, good or bad, does not matter. All that counts is what God has done and is doing. God loves us when we are unlovable and accepts us when we are unacceptable. God's compassion is not put off even by our rebellion. Unless we reject it outright, faith from God fills all the nooks and crannies of our existence which has been faithless. God's grace embraces us in all those moments when divine rejection seems more in order.

Do not try to make sense of it. Paul, the convert from Tarsus, observed that God's wisdom frequently looks like rank foolishness to most of us.

Faith is a most personal matter. But faith is not a private matter. What we receive from God, we are to share with others—love, grace, acceptance. Thus, even in the toughest situations involving anger-inciting relationships, we withhold judgment and bountifully extend mercy. Incidentally, as that happens, we may come off looking as foolish as God's wisdom. And do not think people will not let us know it.

COUNSEL FOR CHURCHES

Churches do need to be singled out for some special words. My deep and abiding love for the church, as a child of the church, does not blind me to correctable faults and meetable needs within the church. Only as the present is reexamined can a better future be anticipated.

The words that follow may seem biased on behalf of ministers. I trust that is not unduly the case. I am well aware that ministers can be scoundrels just like anyone else. Indeed, plenty of documentation is available on ministers who have taken advantage of the congregations they served. Repentance ought not to be a foreign experience to those who from behind pulpits and desks regularly declare to others, "Repent."

But something is wrong in churches. And whatever the problem is, indications are that it is getting worse. "Forced termination" has become a major topic of conversation in every denomination. Resignations from pastorates and dropouts from the ministry are proliferating. (Within the week in which I write, from a neighboring state word has come of five major churches which either have terminated their pastors or received the pressured resignations of their pastors, and from highly publicized stories in the local media news has come of pastoral transitions related to stress and surrounded by controversy in two different denominations.) Frankly, though, those may not be the worst aspects of the story.

A recent report within my own denomination revealed that in the last calendar year, aside from maternity benefits, among pastors more health-insurance money was paid for medical claims arising from stress-related problems than for any other difficulty. And the costliest hospital claims among pastors and their families were for the treatment of psychosis. Something is wrong in pastor-congregation relations.

These words to churches come from one who has known local congregations at their best and at their worst. Within churches, my soul has been sent soaring by worshipful celebrations and my mind has seemed trampled to death by a preoccupation with trivia. In some fellowships of believers my heart has been broken by the pettiness and the prevalence of a deeply disturbed pseudo-piousness, while in others my will has been challenged by an interest in commitment only to a truly biblically defined piety. Here are some suggestions for all people in the family of faith.

Do not ask or allow a minister to marry the church. Efforts to the contrary result in an unholy as well as an inhuman union which quickly will diminish the minister as a person and ultimately be of no benefit to the congregation. Pastor and people as loving participants in the church as a family of faith is a wonderful biblical image. A picture of a minister and a congregation as spouses in wedlock is theologically incorrect and psychologically sick.

Know that the church is the bride of Christ. Every minister is to be a servant of Christ. Christian ordination to the ministry does not require a rejection of intimate relationships with the human family. Both church and pastor will best relate to each other while jointly fulfilling a God-given mission if the biblical identity of each is maintained. Please do not accept the existence of a pastor-congregation relationship that is clearly objectionable ideologically.

Be realistic in your expectations of ministers. One Sunday evening prior to leading a service of worship in a deep-South

city, Carlyle Marney met with the pastoral search committee (then called "pulpit committee") of the congregation.
Having spent an hour listening to members of that committee discuss their expectations for a new pastor, Marney
announced to the worshipers, "I have some good news and
some bad news for you. The good news is that you have a
fine pulpit committee. The bad news is that there are no
more thirty-five-year-old ex-Confederate generals available!"

Ridiculous? Sure. But no more ridiculous than other
pastor-related expectations that never get challenged. ("Our
pastor will help our church to grow numerically, increase its
budget, better supervise the staff, revise its committee
structure, and more efficiently conduct its business. Of
course, our pastor also will need to pay attention to shut-ins,
be present in crises, visit the hospitals, serve as a leader in
the community, be available for counseling, remain
biblically and theologically astute, teach Sunday school
classes, join social functions among the members, and
preach sermons that are powerful, substantive, and short.")
Please do not set up your pastor for failure. Some congregations call a pastor to do the work of several people, to
guarantee what cannot be guaranteed, to serve as a stand-in
for God.

*Remember that perfect pastors are as difficult to find as perfect
parishioners.* Even if you think you have a perfect pastor at
first, be assured you are wrong. Only human beings are
available for the pastorate. Imperfection is a certainty. Expect
mistakes, failures, and sins, and pledge to be understanding,
supportive, and forgiving. Treat your pastor with at least as
much tolerance and care as you would a member of your
human family or a prospective church member known to be
very wealthy.

Realize that no minister, whether pastor or other staff
member, *can meet all your needs or all your church's needs.* In
fact, students of human relations tell us that no one person

can meet all the needs of any other person. Pastors are persons.

Praise your pastor for taking time off as well as for working hard *and for efforts that failed* as well as for programs that succeeded. You can best know your pastor's needs in this regard by looking at your own needs.

Dismiss, desist from, and forget both the language and the attitude of "hiring a pastor." Think and speak of your pastor as a colleague in ministry. Sure, the congregation pays its pastor's salary. A congregation certainly may "fire" a pastor. But no congregation ever should be able to buy a pastor. Prophets and priests are not for hire.

Insist that your pastor participate in regularly scheduled experiences of continuing education and relaxation. Everyone, pastor and congregation, will benefit from these times. If the pastor becomes so busy as to assume such experiences must be delayed or ignored, be a minister-friend and challenge that view. Faithfulness in this area is just as crucial as compliance with any part of a pastor's job description.

Do not promise what cannot be delivered—to the pastor or through the pastor. Honestly brief a prospective pastor on what legitimately can be expected from the congregation. If you cannot be precise, understate, rather than overstate, expected benefits, and overstate, rather than understate, possible problems. Also, please refrain from making a pastor responsible for the fulfillment of unrealistic promises made by the church to the community or to any group of people in it.

Allow the pastor the same freedom enjoyed by others in deciding about sacrifice. Sacrifices should not be imposed on the pastor. The fact that a person functions within a "holy calling" is not an adequate reason to take advantage of that person.

Practice love and grace. As much as possible rid yourselves of the "but" that precedes a compromise of New Testament principles and practices. Refuse to be satisfied with your church or to give yourself to any other priority within your church until your church can exist as a community of love and grace. At stake is your basic identity—the church as just another community agency with commendable programs and services or the church as a fellowship of the people of God. Do not expect the community to understand the depth of your forgiveness, the breadth of your acceptance, or the greatness of your open heart. Of course, a church practicing love and grace is not for the good of the pastor but for obedience to Christ, for the benefit of all who need its ministry, and for the glory of God.

MEMOS TO MINISTERS

My files are full of memos to myself. I like to make notations for future reference—truths to remember, instructions to follow, research to pursue, ideas to consider, questions to answer, plans to implement. Thus, as I have worked my way through the reflections, observations, and evaluations that make up this book, I have written down certain matters to which I want to devote continuing attention. The subject of each memo is highlighted. But the issues under consideration here are larger than any one person and worthy of careful attention from more than only one minister. Thus, the memos that follow are for all who do ministry.

RE: IDENTITY AND INTEGRITY

Be yourself. Avoid acting. Dismiss deception.

So what if you are a minister? That does not make you any less a person or obliterate feelings at emotional extremities or prevent thoughts that defy reason. Denying your humanity will not enhance your ministry.

Remember the price to be paid for repressing anger, covering up disappointments, disguising hurt, faking strength, ignoring guilt, and running from grief. Then claim the freedom to show disappointment, express anger, reveal hurt, confess guilt, admit weakness, and weep with grief.

Emotional deceit—whether directed at yourself or at someone else—destroys integrity as quickly and effectively as speaking a blatant lie. Preserving integrity with honest expressions of identity is far more important than always trying to please everybody encountered and to present a commendable image.

Re.: Reality

You are capable of almost anything. Do not forget it. Probably you have the potential to accomplish a great amount of good. Certainly you have the ability to perpetuate deplorable evil.

Experience indicates that you can get sick without knowing it and in an awful confusion identify wrong as right, hurting as helping, and failing as achieving. Thus you need regular checkups with people who will assist you in dealing with reality. If those persons do not come forward voluntarily, and most likely they will not, seek them out and request their help. You can be a healthy person, but not apart from maintaining a correct understanding and exercising a decisive will related to health.

Profuse denials of reality are not indicative of profound spirituality.

Re.: Work and Worth

You are a person of worth regardless of the nature of your work. Becoming more important professionally neither enhances nor diminishes your value personally.

Personal health—physical, emotional, mental, and spiritual—is more important than job classification and financial income. If the enjoyment of good health requires doing something that means making less money, do it.

Re.: Demythologized Ministry

Ministry is a holy calling, but not all ministers are holy people and not all ministries are carried out for holy purposes. Ministry involves a diverse cross section of people with multiple mixtures of motives.

A minister is a person first. Ministry should make a person more human, not less.

Refrain from repeating the action of the Boy Scout who helped a little old lady across the street when she did not want to go across the street.

Guard carefully your criteria for success and reject all substitutes for faithfulness.

Attempts to play God neither please God nor serve God. Ministers regularly need ministry. No exceptions.

Pray to God often and be alert to your own responsibilities for self-protection.

Re.: Devotion to the Church

Maintain a high view of the church. Do not let anyone talk you out of commitment to the biblical image of the church. Acknowledge, though, that any local expression of the church is an institution filled with human beings who are imperfect and sinful like yourself.

Remember the indications of Scripture and the lessons of history that holy causes can, and often do, get awfully sick. When that happens, they need to be treated as sick.

Self-centeredness is easily disguised in the church. Likewise, manipulation can be covered by conversations heavy on God-talk. You do not have to be nice to rank meanness within the church any more than you have to succumb to meanness anywhere else, even if the meanness in the church is mistakenly called righteousness.

Do not expect a congregation of people to act like the church if they do not understand the New Testament meaning of the church.

Keep the worth of the church in proper perspective. Not all the flaws in the world can compromise the importance of the church's mission to people in need and the value of the church's worship of God.

Do not forget that the church belongs to God and not God to the church. Thus, seek first to serve God even if a particular church thinks that such service is not in its best interest.

Re.: Substance and Show

Do not get sucked into culture's fascination with show, indeed, its elevation of show over substance. Do not allow symbols—the right office, an impressive title, correct attire, appropriate recognition—to mean too much to you. To be fulfilled personally and productive professionally you do not have to be properly dressed in a business suit (coat on), seated behind a big desk in a protected study with your name on the door, and have a skilled secretary in an outer office. (Incidentally, most of this book was written while seated at the kitchen table, dressed in casual slacks or shorts and a pullover shirt.)

Re.: Personal Relationships

Make intimacy at home a high priority. Seek continuous growth in your understanding of intimacy and then act on what is known.

Commit yourself to a few friendships. Work at them conscientiously. Do not expect many good friends, and do not be disappointed if some of the people you thought to be good friends fail at times. Refuse to permit failures among your friends to justify your lack of efforts to maintain fidelity as a friend to them. Be the very best friend you can be.

Accept the fact that you cannot be intimate or even close friends with everybody. Do try, though, to be sensitive to all the people you meet.

Give thanks to God for good relationships. They are among God's very best gifts.

RE.: RUMORS

Refuse to be a recipient or a conduit of rumors.

Do not pass along to others un-checked-out information. If you cannot verify the truth of a matter, drop the matter.

Challenge people who delight in sowing seeds of suspicion and whispering "confidential" observations that could hurt another individual.

RE.: MINIMIZING JUDGMENT

Obey the commandment (not suggestion) of Jesus that reverberates through the writings of the New Testament: "Judge not."

Face facts. You are as incapable of judging the behavior or character of other people as they are of judging you. Do not even attempt such judgment. If for some reason you think through words of judgment about someone, do not give voice to them.

Work toward the day when you will not find delight when those who have judged you become the brunts of the judgment or punishment of others.

How can people who worship God sincerely think of playing God by assuming the divine prerogative of passing judgment?

RE.: MAXIMIZING GRACE

Continue to study the nature and role of grace in the Scriptures so as to know more how to incarnate grace in the various experiences of your life. Concentrate on demonstrating grace to people who neither understand its primacy nor appreciate its ministry.

Do not deny yourself the same grace you extend to others.

Remember that God's grace can overcome anything— anything, that is, except the willful rejection of it.

Re.: Feeding the Spirit

Do not get so busy that you cannot spend some time frivolously, read a novel that will make no contribution to you except the pleasure of pondering its plot, unhurriedly stand before a painting soaking up its beauty and reveling in the artist's creativity, go out to dinner with family members or friends and not look at your watch a single time during the evening.

Stay alert to opportunities for fun. Assign a high priority to claiming such times with a vigor equal to that devoted to work.

Read some poetry regularly.

At times listen only to music you like, not music the people around you say you should enjoy.

Keep in mind the pleasure of a picnic, a barefoot walk along that part of a beach where the waves wash up to cover your ankles with water, "wasting" time sitting on a bench talking to one of your children or some other favorite person.

Schedule rendezvous with joy, but be ready to lay hold of diversions of delight at a moment's notice.

Keep in proper perspective the criticisms of those who label such counsel (even to oneself) as out-of-touch romanticism.

Re.: Hope

Personally, hoping that the worst of times are past and that depression will not become debilitating again, I am strengthened by the assurance that the hope I have found where I have been will be available wherever I am (you are) and however I am (you are) in the future.

The substance of confident hope resides not in what you can do but in what God can do with what you do and with you.

Epilogue

Writing and reading about the past can be tricky. Looking back, a totality can be seen to experiences—patterns, diversions, regressions, reasons, progressions—that is an impossibility as they occur. Subsequently, as the whole of an episode is studied, the powerful significance of individual aspects of it may be missed. Especially if the period of history considered has a positive conclusion, "a happy ending," many of the negatives involved in it—actual pain, unresolved hostilities, rubbed-raw emotions, troubling unanswered questions, shattered relationships—go ignored. Or if not ignored, not sensitively understood. The positive surge of patriotism and thrilling sensations of glory prompted by reading about a wartime battle often miss the repulsive aspects of the event—the trauma of seeing a friend shredded by shrapnel, an explosion of indescribable fear, a frantic desire for personal security and a reunion with family members, and the horror induced by a chaotic spectacle of sickening gore.

Though I have labored at candor in this volume, events with jagged edges that have hurt like splinters in the quick, disgusting conversations, nauseating stretches of anxiety, days of grinding despair have been left undescribed. Fortunately, in my experience some really bad moments have led to some very good moments and the promise of more. But all of the pilgrimage should be taken into account. If anyone can read this material and, because of an affinity with the positives that have emerged, think, That's not so bad; I think I would not mind enduring such a time of pain to get to such a situation of improved health—that person has been tricked severely by illusions of neatness and conciseness which often accompany a consideration of distant developments.

Yes, some new, badly needed levels of maturity resulted from moments (which often seemed like eternities) when life was in disarray, from a period of hospitalization which was very helpful, and from dealing with innumerable difficulties which resulted in discovering previously ignored resources and strengthening capacities for joy—for me. Would I recommend my journey to others? No! (That is an emphatic negative.) Would I choose to go through it all again in order to discover the benefits derived from it? No! (Again, emphatically.) Health can be, but does not have to be, achieved only after sickness has been experienced. Sensitivity, emotional integrity, liberty, and intimacy can be developed much more intentionally, wisely, and normally.

Whether or not I could have avoided depression altogether remains an open question in my mind. But some of the conditions and situations that worsened it and continued it (if not caused it) could have been avoided. That is by far the better way.

My words are in no sense intended as an encouragement for others to share my experiences. God forbid! Rather, what I have hoped to set down in print are caution flags or stop signs, to get the attention of and perhaps to alter the course of persons who see themselves descending into a similar valley. And my reflections are shared as hints of hope for persons presently in the darkness. Light can dawn again. A better future is a possibility. I know.

The materials in this volume are autobiographical. However, the book is by no means a complete autobiography. A decade of depression is not the whole story of my life. Prior to these days, positives abounded amid a few negatives. Sorrow, conflict, and discouragement were encountered, to be sure. But, at times, experiences seemed almost too good to be true.

Though I have written the conclusion to this volume, the story of my days is not ended. The present is very pleasant. Familially, Judy and I are finding enjoyment in an enriched relationship with each other and a more studied approach to engagements with others. Priority is given to spontaneous and lighthearted fun. Important segments of time are claimed for togetherness with our boys. Thankfully, I sense that I am once again making some important contributions to the family. Socially, I am trying to practice more honesty —accepting invitations, scheduling appointments, and attending functions because I want to rather than because I have to. More important than ever are extended moments of relaxed conversation—casual and serious—with people who can be trusted completely, friends for whom and from whom care is unconditional. Professionally, I have not yet accepted a permanent position. Predictably, that has its problems financially. But I am thoroughly enjoying involvement in a variety of ministries for totally nonremunerative purposes—not doing ministry to "make a living," but choosing ministry as one of the purposes of living. I can see clearly that a good salary apart from meaningfulness, fulfillment, and happiness is no measure of a good job. Personally, I am at peace. I realize that in all these realms much more has changed within me than has changed around me. I am committed to making whatever additional changes are needed. Good health really is a cause for great gratitude to God!

What does the future hold? I can no more answer that question today than I could have responded accurately to a similar inquiry ten years ago. Maybe that inability to know the future is one of the greatest gifts of God's grace in any present.

Painfully, I am aware of tendencies in my life that can be

terribly hurtful and destructive. Not all of these have been miraculously extracted. However, wisdom born in anguish can assist me in maintaining a constant vigilance to keep such negatives in check. Priorities are better ordered now, though work habits still have to be monitored. Emotional honesty and wholistic intimacy are no easier for me than they ever were, but they are much more important to me. Realistically, I am aware that depression and the plethora of bad experiences which contributed to it, accompanied it, and resulted from it can recur. But I also know the happiness that attends the present rediscovery of health. Born of that realization are a determination to pursue a better way and the conviction that such a different pilgrimage is possible.

Jacob, in the Genesis account of the Old Testament, especially after his experience at Jabbok ford, is my spiritual brother. This ancient Hebrew spent an entire night in a wrestling match with one whom he first recognized as an angel and later identified as God. My struggle has been more of a tag team event. Just as I finished one match, some clanging bell signaled the start of another. Winning or losing, the opponents whom I encountered kept exchanging places in the ring, each one appearing with more vigor than the previous one. During this bout, I believe at one time or another I have wrestled with everybody.

Jacob took a beating, not as an innocent victim but as a responsible participant. Ironically, but not uniquely, his losing was a form of winning. In weakness he discovered strength. Even with a thigh out of joint he was more of a whole person than he was when the dark night began.

Predictably, I identify most with what I like most in this biblical narrative. That is the ending—the ending that is a new beginning. As Jacob is silhouetted against the horizon, his back now turned to the Jabbok from which he is moving on, he is limping. He is limping. But the sun is rising. A new day is dawning.

Let it be, gracious God, let it be.